HOUGHTON MIFFLIN HARCOURT

ARKANSAS JOURNEYS

Program Authors

James F. Baumann · David J. Chard · Jamal Cooks
J. David Cooper · Russell Gersten · Marjorie Lipson
Lesley Mandel Morrow · John J. Pikulski · Héctor H. Rivera
Mabel Rivera · Shane Templeton · Sheila W. Valencia
Catherine Valentino · MaryEllen Vogt

Consulting Author
Irene Fountas

HOUGHTON MIFFLIN HARCOURT

HOUGHTON MIFFLIN HARCOURT

ARKANSAS
JOURNEYS

HOUGHTON MIFFLIN HARCOURT

EXTREMENATURE

Big Idea Our world is an amazing place!

Unit 5

Going Places

💡 **Big Idea** There are many reasons to take a journey.

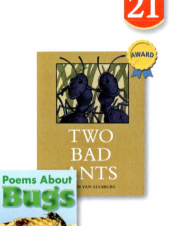
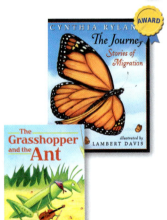

EXTREME NATURE

NATURE

Unit 4

Big Idea

Our world is an amazing place!

Paired Selections

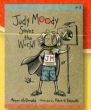

recycle

project

dripping

carton

complicated

pollution

rubbish

hardly

shade

global

Vocabulary
Reader

Context
Cards

Vocabulary in Context

1 recycle
When people recycle old bottles, the glass can be used again.

2 project
This garden is a neighborhood project. Many people work on it.

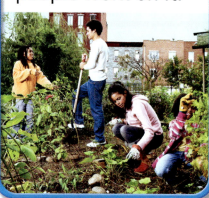

3 dripping
This faucet is dripping water. Each drop of water is wasted.

4 carton
A carton, or light cardboard container, can be recycled after use.

- Study each **Context Card**.
- Make up a new context sentence that uses two Vocabulary words.

5 complicated

One **complicated**, or difficult, part of recycling can be sorting plastic.

6 pollution

Noise **pollution**, or too many loud sounds, can be bad for our hearing.

NO HORN HONKING $350 FINE

7 rubbish

The more **rubbish**, or trash, people make, the more room it takes up.

8 hardly

Some light bulbs use a lot of energy. This bulb uses **hardly** any energy.

9 shade

The **shade** from this tree keeps the house cool in the summer.

10 global

Air pollution is a **global** problem. It affects people all over the world.

Background

Don't Dump It Some towns burn **rubbish**, but burning waste causes air **pollution**. Other towns bury trash, but there is **hardly** any room left in landfills. Too much trash is a **global** problem. The solution is not **complicated**. People need to **recycle**! Make recycling a family **project**. Rinse and sort those **dripping** bottles and cans into bins. Flatten that **carton** and tie it up with newspapers. Recycle kitchen scraps by making compost. It will become fertilizer for your garden.

How to Compost

1. Green yard waste, fruit and vegetable scraps, coffee grounds, tea leaves

2. Dry leaves, straw, sawdust, wood chips, dried grass, shredded cardboard or newspaper

3. Moist soil, ash, fertilizer

Compost in the sun, not the **shade**. Add water and mix the pile every now and then to give it air.

Comprehension

Author's Purpose

Story details give clues about why the author wrote "A Mr. Rubbish Mood." They also give clues to help you figure out the author's theme, or message. Use a chart like this to list details that give clues about the theme. Use the clues to write in your own words what the theme is.

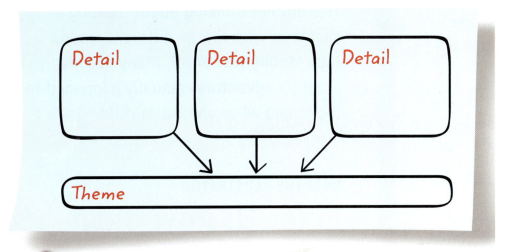

Detail   Detail   Detail

Theme

✓ **TARGET STRATEGY** **Monitor/Clarify**

As you read, monitor and clarify any story details that are unclear. Understanding these details can help you figure out the author's purpose and the theme.

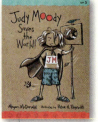

recycle	pollution
project	rubbish
dripping	hardly
carton	shade
complicated	global

Author's Purpose Use text details to tell why an author writes a book.

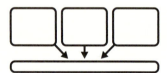

Monitor/Clarify As you read, find a way to clear up what doesn't make sense.

GENRE

Humorous fiction is a story written to entertain readers. Who is the narrator in this story, the author or a story character? How would the story change if it were told from a different point of view?

MEET THE AUTHOR

Megan McDonald

Once while Megan McDonald was visiting a school, some students asked her, "Are you ever in a bad mood?" This got her thinking about creating a character with lots of different moods. Judy Moody was born! Many of Judy Moody's adventures actually happened to McDonald when she was a child.

MEET THE ILLUSTRATOR

Peter H. Reynolds

Peter Reynolds and his twin brother started writing their own books when they were about seven. Reynolds has been drawing and telling stories ever since. After illustrating more than seven Judy Moody books, he feels like Judy Moody's family is part of his own family.

A Mr. Rubbish Mood

from Judy Moody Saves the World!

by **Megan McDonald**
illustrated by **Peter H. Reynolds**

It was still dark out when Judy woke up early the next morning. She found her flashlight and notebook. Then she tiptoed downstairs to the kitchen and started to save the world.

She hoped she could save the world before breakfast. Judy wondered if other people making the world a better place had to do it quietly, and in the dark, so their parents would not wake up.

She, Judy Moody, was in a Mr. Rubbish mood. Mr. Rubbish was the Good Garbage Gremlin in her brother Stink's comic book, who built his house out of French-fry cartons and pop bottles. He recycled everything, even lollipop sticks. And he never used anything from the rain forest.

Hmmm . . . things that came from the rain forest. That would be a good place to start. Rubber came from the rain forest. And chocolate and spices and things like perfume. Even chewing gum.

Judy collected stuff from around the house and piled it on the kitchen table. Chocolate bars, brownie mix, vanilla ice cream. Her dad's coffee beans. The rubber toilet plunger. Gum from Stink's gumball machine. Her mom's lipstick from the bottom of her purse. She was so busy saving the rain forest that she didn't hear her family come into the kitchen.

"What in the world . . . ?" Mom said.

"Judy, why are you in the dark?" Dad asked, turning on the lights.

"Hey, my gumball machine!" Stink said.

Judy held out her arms to block the way. "We're not going to use this stuff anymore. It's all from the rain forest," she told them.

"Says who?" asked Stink.

"Says Mr. Rubbish. They cut down way too many trees to grow coffee and give us makeup and chewing gum. The earth is our home. We have to take action to save it. We don't need all this stuff."

"I need gum!" yelled Stink. "Give me back my gum!"

"Stink! Don't yell. Haven't you ever heard of noise pollution?"

"Is my coffee in there?" Dad asked, rubbing his hair.

"Judy? Is that ice cream? It's dripping all over the table!" Mom carried the leaky carton over to the sink.

"ZZZZ-ZZZZZ!" Judy made the sound of a chain saw cutting down trees.

"She's batty," Stink said.

Dad put the brownie mix back in the cupboard. Mom took the toilet plunger off the kitchen table and headed for the bathroom.

Time for Plan B. Project R.E.C.Y.C.L.E. She, Judy Moody, would show her family just how much they hurt the planet. Every time someone threw something away, she would write it down. She got her notebook and looked in the trash can. She wrote down:

1 orange juice can
1 inside of peanut butter jar lid
1 plastic bread bag
4 broken eggshells
smelly yucky wet coffee grounds
3 paper muffin holders
2 smooshed Scarlett O'cherry juice boxes (and straws!)
½ bowl of oatmeal

"Stink! You shouldn't throw gooey old oatmeal in the trash!" Judy said.

"Dad! Tell her to quit spying on me."

"I'm a Garbage Detective!" said Judy. "*Garbologist* to you. If you want to learn what to recycle, you have to get to know your garbage."

"Here," said Stink, sticking something wet and mushy under Judy's nose. "Get to know my apple core."

"Hardee-har-har," said Judy. "Hasn't anybody in this family ever heard of the Three R's?"

"The Three R's?" asked Dad.

"Re-use. Re-cycle."

"What's the third one?" asked Stink.

"Re-fuse to talk to little brothers until they quit throwing stuff away."

"Mom! I'm not going to stop throwing stuff away just because Judy's having a trash attack."

"Look at all this stuff we throw away!" Judy said. "Did you know that one person throws away more than eight pounds of garbage a day?"

"We recycle all our glass and cans," said Mom.

"And newspapers," Dad said.

"But what about this?" said Judy, picking a plastic bag out of the trash. "This bread bag could be a purse! Or carry a library book."

STOP AND THINK

Author's Craft The word *gooey* on page 22 is an example of onomatopoeia. Find another example of onomatopoeia on page 22.

"What's so great about eggshells?" asked Stink. "And smelly old ground-up coffee?"

"You can use them to feed plants. Or make compost." Just then, something in the trash caught her eye. A pile of wooden craft sticks? Judy pulled it out. "Hey! My Laura Ingalls Wilder log cabin I made in second grade!"

"It looks like a glue museum to me," said Stink.

"I'm sorry, Judy," Mom said. "I should have asked first, but we can't save everything, honey."

"Recycle it!" said Stink. "You could use it for kindling, to start a fire! Or break it down in toothpicks."

"Not funny, Stink."

"Judy, you're not even ready for school yet. Let's talk about this later," said Dad. "It's time to get dressed."

It was no use. Nobody listened to her. Judy trudged upstairs, feeling like a sloth without a tree.

"I won't wear lipstick today if it'll make you feel better," Mom called up the stairs.

"And I'll only drink half a cup of coffee," Dad said, but Judy could hardly hear him over the grinding of the rain forest coffee beans.

STOP AND THINK

Monitor/Clarify Does Stink believe Judy should use her log cabin for kindling or toothpicks, or is there another reason he said this?

Her family sure knew how to ruin a perfectly good Mr. Rubbish mood. She put on her jeans and her Spotted Owl T-shirt. And to save water, she did not brush her teeth.

She clomped downstairs in a mad-at-your-whole-family mood.

"Here's your lunch," said Mom.

"Mom! It's in a paper bag!"

"What's wrong with that?" Stink asked.

"Don't you get it?" said Judy. "They cut down trees to make paper bags. Trees give shade. They help control global warming. We would die without trees. They make oxygen and help take dust and stuff out of the air."

"Dust!" said Mom. "Let's talk about cleaning your room if we're going to talk about dust."

"Mo-om!" How was she supposed to do important things like save trees if she couldn't even save her *family* tree? That did it. Judy went straight to the garage and dug out her Sleeping Beauty lunch box from kindergarten.

STOP AND THINK

Author's Purpose Who is more convincing in the story, Judy or her family? What might this tell you about the author's opinion of recycling?

"Are you really going to take that baby lunch box on the bus? Where the whole world can see?" asked Stink.

"I'm riding my bike today," said Judy. "To save energy."

"See you at school, then." Stink waved his *paper-bag* lunch at her. If only she could recycle her little brother.

"Go ahead. Be a tree hater," called Judy.

Making the world a better place sure was complicated.

Your Turn

Dear Judy

Write an E-Mail Saving the world isn't an easy job. Imagine that you are Judy's friend. What advice would you give her about her plans to protect the environment? Write your ideas in an e-mail to Judy. PERSONAL RESPONSE

Be a Garbologist

Make a List With a partner, make a list of all the things you throw away or recycle in one day. Next to each item, list whether you could reduce or reuse it. Discuss how you could do so. PARTNERS

Funny Business

Turn and Talk Sometimes authors write stories for more than one reason. With a partner, discuss why you think Megan MacDonald wrote *A Mr. Rubbish Mood.* Why do you think she made it a funny story instead of a serious one?

AUTHOR'S PURPOSE

✓ TARGET VOCABULARY

recycle	pollution
project	rubbish
dripping	hardly
carton	shade
complicated	global

GENRE

Informational text gives factual information about a topic. This is a magazine article.

TEXT FOCUS

Headings are titles for different parts of a selection. Look at the headings in this article. What do you think the article will be about? After you read, see if your predictions were correct.

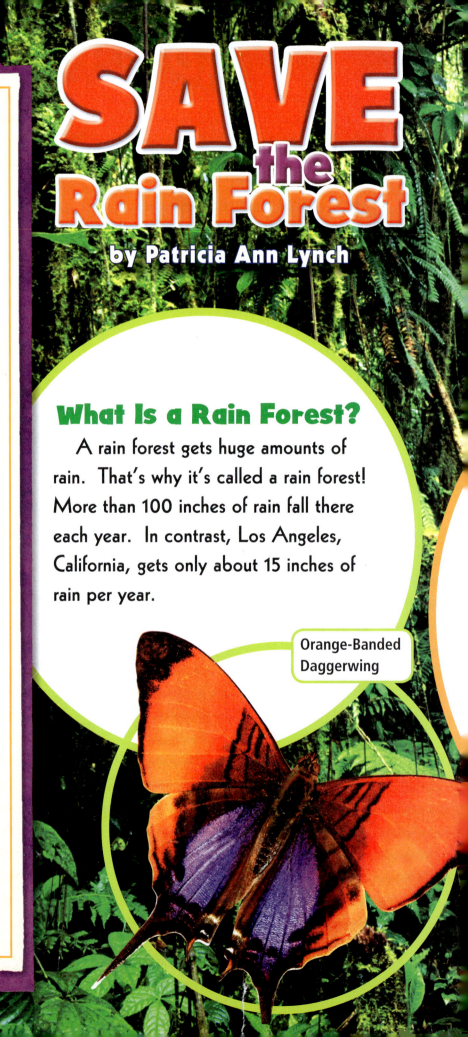

SAVE the Rain Forest

by Patricia Ann Lynch

What Is a Rain Forest?

A rain forest gets huge amounts of rain. That's why it's called a rain forest! More than 100 inches of rain fall there each year. In contrast, Los Angeles, California, gets only about 15 inches of rain per year.

Orange-Banded Daggerwing

Toco Toucan

Rain Forest Plants

A rain forest has hundreds of kinds of trees and flowers. Under your feet is a carpet of leaves. Moisture is dripping everywhere. Hardly any light reaches the ground because tall trees form a canopy, or upper layer, high above. It hides the sky and provides shade.

Rain Forest Animals

A rain forest is noisy! Birds squawk. Thousands of insects buzz and hum. Monkeys chatter in the trees. Beetles grow as big as your hand. Some frogs grow as big as a milk carton!

Red-Eyed Leaf Frog

Why Are Rain Forests in Trouble?

Rain forests are important to life on Earth. They recycle. Tree roots use dead plants as food. Rain turns into clouds that make more rain. Trees take in carbon dioxide and give off the air we breathe.

Yet rain forests are in trouble. People cut down trees to get wood and land to farm. Most trees are not replaced. Many scientists think this may be a cause of global warming. Loggers also may leave rubbish behind. This is a kind of pollution.

The balance of life in a rain forest is complicated. Plants and animals depend on one another. If one dies out, others do, too.

Golden-Browed Chlorophonia

The Children's Rain Forest

In 1987, children in a Swedish school were studying rain forests. They learned that rain forests were in trouble. The class started a project to save a rain forest in Costa Rica. The class bought about 15 acres of land. This was the start of the Children's Rain Forest. This project works to save rain forests around the world.

Harvested logs in an Indonesian rain forest

Making Connections

Text to Self

Talk About Helping In *A Mr. Rubbish Mood*, Judy Moody reduces the use of rain forest products. Take turns in a group telling about something you do or would like to do to help the environment. Ask questions to learn more about each person's ideas.

Text to Text

Write a Letter In *A Mr. Rubbish Mood* and "Save the Rain Forest," you read about ways to save the rain forests. Write a letter to the editor of a newspaper that tells readers why the rain forests are in danger and three ways they can help.

Text to World

Connect to Social Studies Research the locations of rain forests around the world. Show the class where the rain forests are by pointing to them on a map.

Grammar

What Is an Adjective? An **adjective** is a word that describes, or tells about, a noun. Some adjectives tell what kind. Some tell how many.

Adjective
I recycle **old** cans.
A **plastic** bin holds the cans.
Nine cans are in the bin now.

Turn and Talk **Work with a partner. Read each sentence aloud. Identify the adjective in each sentence.**

1. A loud noise awakened Tanya.

2. Giant bottles were singing in Tanya's room!

3. They were telling Tanya to recycle old bottles.

4. Tanya tried many times to go back to sleep.

5. Today she will recycle fifty bottles.

Sentence Fluency You can make your writing smooth and clear if you combine some sentences. If two short sentences tell about one noun, try combining the sentences by moving an adjective.

Short Sentences

Our town has its own recycling bins.

The bins are green.

Longer, Smoother Sentence

Our town has its own green recycling bins.

Connect Grammar to Writing

As you revise your persuasive letter, try moving adjectives to combine sentences.

Write to Persuade

✅ **Ideas** In *Judy Moody Saves the World*, Judy gives strong reasons for saving trees. When you revise your **persuasive letter**, think about the reasons you gave for your goal. Will they seem important to your reader?

Bianca wrote a letter persuading her neighbors to do more walking. Later, she changed some of her reasons to make them stronger.

Writing Traits Checklist

✅ **Ideas**
Did I state my goal and give strong reasons?

✅ **Organization**
Did I use correct letter form?

✅ **Word Choice**
Did I use polite language?

✅ **Voice**
Did I write in a positive tone?

✅ **Sentence Fluency**
Did I combine short, choppy sentences?

✅ **Conventions**
Did I use commas correctly? Did I write neatly in cursive?

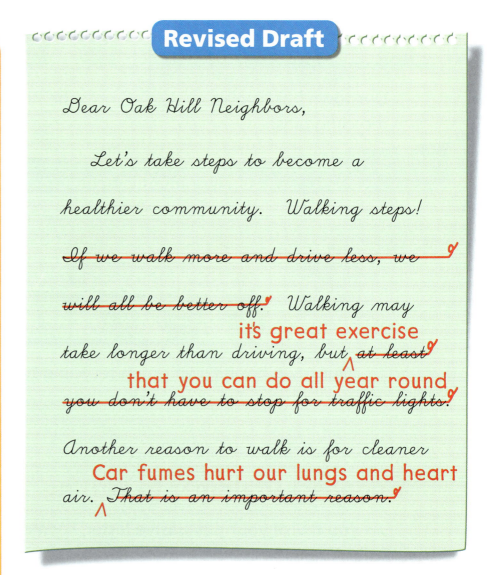

Revised Draft

Dear Oak Hill Neighbors,

Let's take steps to become a healthier community. Walking steps!

~~If we walk more and drive less, we will all be better off.~~ Walking may take longer than driving, but ~~at least~~ it's great exercise that you can do all year round ~~you don't have to stop for traffic lights.~~

Another reason to walk is for cleaner air. Car fumes hurt our lungs and heart ~~That is an important reason.~~

36

182 Foster Street

Bentley, MO 23456

April 8, 2009

Oak Hill Neighborhood Organization

15 Cherry Street

Bentley, MO 23456

Dear Oak Hill Neighbors,

Let's take steps to become a healthier community. Walking steps! Walking may take longer than driving, but it's great exercise that you can do all year round. Another important reason to walk is for cleaner air. Car fumes hurt our lungs and heart. Finally, walking is relaxing because you can chat with neighbors and enjoy being outside. Let's all walk more for a healthier, happier community.

Sincerely,

Bianca Romano

> I gave strong reasons for my goal. I also combined two short sentences.

Reading as a Writer

Which sentence states Bianca's goal? Are the reasons important? Where can you give stronger reasons in your letter?

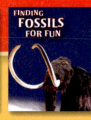

fossils

clues

remains

prove

evidence

skeletons

uncovering

buried

fierce

location

Vocabulary
Reader

Context
Cards

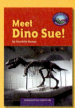

Vocabulary in Context

1 fossils

This man has found dinosaur **fossils**. He will learn a lot from the old bones.

2 clues

Fossils give **clues** that help scientists solve mysteries about dinosaurs.

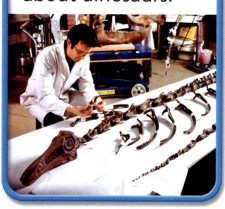

3 remains

These are the **remains** of a large dinosaur. One bone is all that is left.

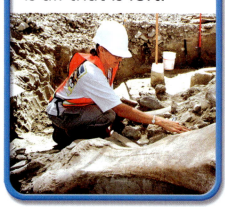

4 prove

Scientists are trying to **prove**, or show, that dinosaurs and birds are related.

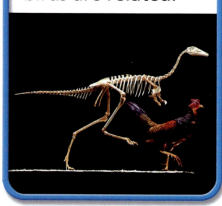

- Study each **Context Card**.
- Ask a question that uses one of the Vocabulary words.

5 evidence

Egg fossils give **evidence**, or facts, about how dinosaurs raised their young.

6 skeletons

Scientists rarely find whole dinosaur **skeletons** like this one.

7 uncovering

Uncovering fossils takes time. The soil must be removed from around them.

8 buried

Many dinosaur bones **buried**, or covered, in mud turned into fossils.

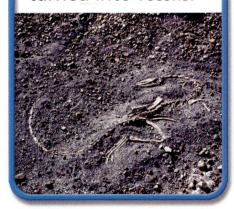

9 fierce

Many people think of dinosaurs as **fierce** animals that fought all the time.

10 location

Sometimes many dinosaur bones are found in the same **location**.

Background

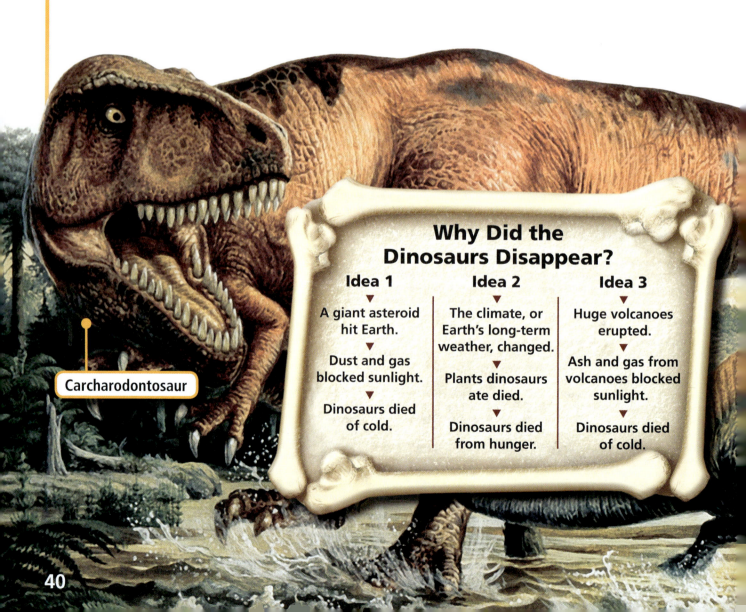

✔ **TARGET VOCABULARY** **Dig and Discover** Paleontologists are like science detectives. They use dinosaur **fossils buried** in the ground as **clues** to solve mysteries. Each new fossil provides **evidence** to help **prove** ideas, such as whether a dinosaur was **fierce** or gentle.

Sometimes paleontologists are lucky and find entire **skeletons** in a single **location**. Other times the **remains** of a creature may be only a few bones or teeth. Scientists can learn more about the past by **uncovering** fossils.

Carcharodontosaur

Why Did the Dinosaurs Disappear?

Idea 1	Idea 2	Idea 3
▼	▼	▼
A giant asteroid hit Earth.	The climate, or Earth's long-term weather, changed.	Huge volcanoes erupted.
▼	▼	▼
Dust and gas blocked sunlight.	Plants dinosaurs ate died.	Ash and gas from volcanoes blocked sunlight.
▼	▼	▼
Dinosaurs died of cold.	Dinosaurs died from hunger.	Dinosaurs died of cold.

Comprehension

✔ **TARGET SKILL**   **Conclusions**

As you read *The Albertosaurus Mystery*, use text clues to draw conclusions, or make smart guesses, about what it's like to be a fossil hunter. Write text clues in a chart like this. Then use the text clues to help you draw a conclusion.

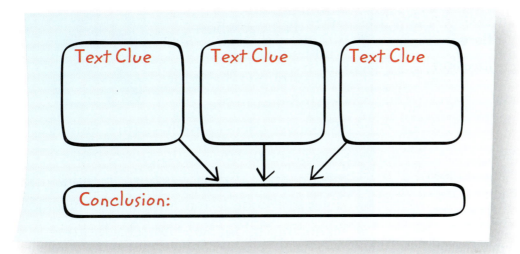

✔ **TARGET STRATEGY**   **Visualize**

Use details from *The Albertosaurus Mystery* to help you visualize, or picture, what the author describes. Then draw conclusions about what it's like to hunt fossils.

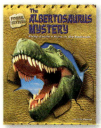

✔ TARGET VOCABULARY

fossils	skeletons
clues	uncovering
remains	buried
prove	fierce
evidence	location

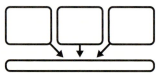

✔ TARGET SKILL

Conclusions Use text details to figure out ideas the author doesn't state.

✔ TARGET STRATEGY

Visualize As you read, use selection details to picture what is happening.

GENRE

Informational text gives factual information about a topic.

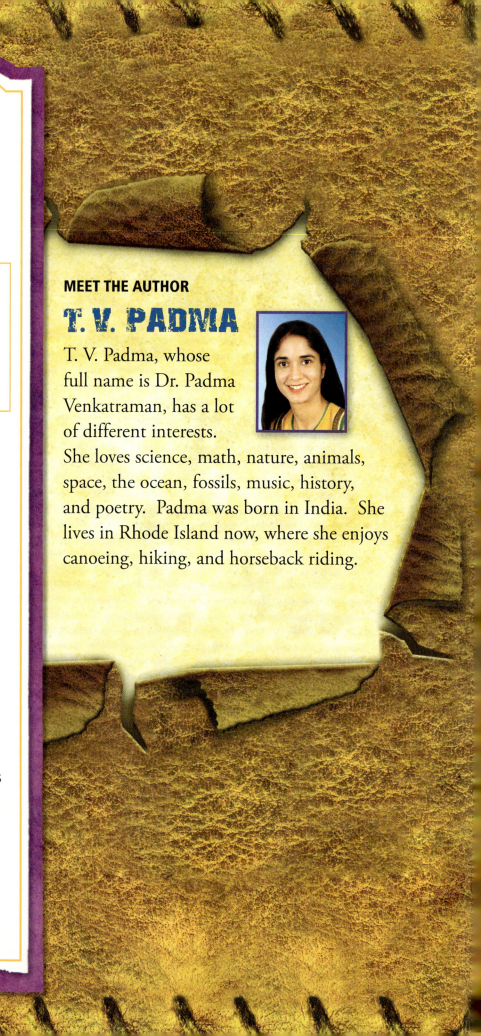

MEET THE AUTHOR

T. V. PADMA

T. V. Padma, whose full name is Dr. Padma Venkatraman, has a lot of different interests. She loves science, math, nature, animals, space, the ocean, fossils, music, history, and poetry. Padma was born in India. She lives in Rhode Island now, where she enjoys canoeing, hiking, and horseback riding.

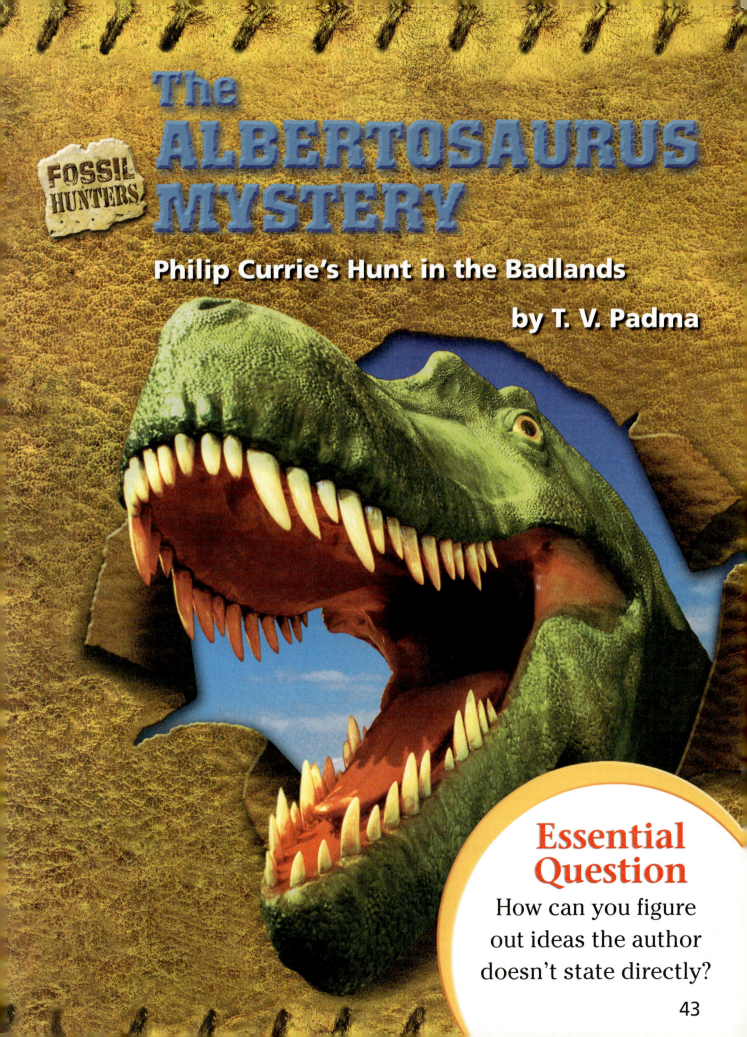

The ALBERTOSAURUS MYSTERY

FOSSIL HUNTERS

Philip Currie's Hunt in the Badlands

by T. V. Padma

Essential Question

How can you figure out ideas the author doesn't state directly?

Searching Without a Map

Many fossils are buried in Canada's badlands. More than 40 kinds of dinosaurs once lived there.

Philip Currie was thirsty and tired. It was one of the hottest summer days of 1997. He and his team were looking for fossils that belonged to a dinosaur called *Albertosaurus* (al bur toh SOHR uhs).

The badlands of western Canada are full of hills. Philip didn't know which hill held Brown's fossils.

Almost 90 years earlier, a famous fossil hunter named Barnum Brown had found a fossil field in western Canada's badlands. Many albertosaurs were buried in it. Philip was trying to find this place again.

It was like looking for a needle in a haystack. Brown had not made a map or written down where he had found the fossils. Philip had few clues—just some notes and four old photos.

Discovery!

The team was running out of water. Everyone except Philip went back to the camp. He continued on with the search. Sand flies and mosquitoes bit him. His head hurt.

Philip had seen the ==remains== of Brown's campsite earlier in the day. He knew the bones must be close.

STOP AND THINK

Author's Craft Why does the author use short, choppy sentences on this page?

Philip was trying to find the ==location== of *Albertosaurus* fossils shown in Brown's old photograph.

All alone, Philip climbed another hill. He stopped to hold up a photo. It looked just like the scene in front of him. He also could see that years ago someone had dug into the rock there. Philip had found Brown's bone bed!

Brown's photo was old, but Philip could see that the hills still looked the same.

Holes or cuts in rocky hills are clues that someone might have dug there before.

Barnum the Bone Hunter

Barnum Brown grew up in Kansas in the late 1800s. His family dug and sold coal. Young Barnum saw his first fossil when the family plow accidentally pulled one out of the ground.

Brown went on to study fossils. He found that he liked digging up bones more than learning about them in class. So he left Columbia University to become a bone hunter for the American Museum of Natural History in New York City.

Brown was very good at finding fossils. Henry Fairfield Osborn, the head of the museum, joked that Brown could "smell fossils." News writers called him "Mr. Bones."

At the American Museum of Natural History in New York City, Brown helped put together the bones he found.

Finding the First T. rex

In 1908, Brown found this *T. rex* skeleton. It can be seen at the American Museum of Natural History.

In the early 1900s, Brown dug up *Tyrannosaurus rex* (tuh ran uh SOHR uhs REKS) skeletons, first in Wyoming, and later in Montana. These were the first *T. rex* skeletons ever found.

For several years, Brown returned to Montana to dig for fossils. The bones he found there were often stuck in hard rock. He sometimes used dynamite to get them out.

Then in 1910 a terrible thing happened in Brown's life. His wife died. Brown tried to forget his sadness by hunting for more fossils. He rafted down Red Deer River Canyon in Canada. He camped in the area, and looked for bones. Soon, Brown made a surprising discovery.

Finding Many Meat-Eaters

In Canada, Brown found a place where many skeletons were buried. The skeletons belonged to *Albertosaurus*, a large meat-eating dinosaur. It was the first time anyone had found the bones of so many meat-eating dinosaurs in the same spot.

Brown dug up some of the bones. He wrote only a few lines about his find but didn't say how unusual it was. He didn't say why he thought so many individuals of the same species were together. He didn't tell what this discovery might mean.

The *Albertosaurus* bones were sent to the museum and put away. There they lay in a basement storage room for many years with other dinosaur fossils.

Albertosaurus got its name because the dinosaur's fossils were first found in Alberta, Canada.

A Fierce Family

Albertosaurus was part of a family of <mark>fierce</mark>, meat-eating dinosaurs called tyrannosaurids. *Tyrannosaurus rex* was also part of this family.

Albertosaurus was smaller than *Tyrannosaurus rex*, but it was strong. *Albertosaurus* could see and smell well. It had many sharp teeth. Its huge, powerful jaws could crush bone.

Like *Tyrannosaurus rex*, *Albertosaurus* lived and hunted alone. At least, that's what paleontologists thought. One man was about to change their thinking, however. He had some ideas about these ancient creatures.

STOP AND THINK

Visualize What words and phrases help you visualize how *Albertosaurus* looked and acted?

Tyrannosaurus rex was about 40 feet (12 meters) long. *Albertosaurus* was about 30 feet (9 meters) long.

Philip Currie's Question

In 1976, Philip Currie read what Brown wrote about the site full of albertosaurs. At that time, most paleontologists thought tyrannosaurids lived alone. If so, asked Philip, why were many of these animals buried together? Had they died together? Had they lived together?

Some plant-eating dinosaurs had lived in groups. Maybe some of the meat-eaters that hunted them did, too, thought Philip. After all, big groups of animals were hard to hunt alone. Maybe albertosaurs hunted in packs.

Philip was busy learning about many kinds of fossils and dinosaurs, however. He put his questions away for many years, just as Brown had put away his fossils.

Albertosaurus **had about seventy teeth in its gigantic jaws.**

The Bones in the Basement

◀ The American Museum of Natural History, where Brown's *Albertosaurus* fossils were stored.

This fossil foot bone from an *Albertosaurus* was first discovered by Barnum Brown in Alberta, Canada, and then rediscovered by Philip Currie in New York City. ▶

Philip thought about his questions again 20 years later. This time, however, something happened that made him hunt for answers.

Philip came across some *Albertosaurus* bones in the basement of the American Museum of Natural History—the museum where Barnum Brown had worked. He could tell that the bones were from the badlands in Canada where Brown had been searching for fossils.

Philip saw that Brown had found at least nine albertosaurs in one spot. He also saw that Brown had taken only a few bones from each animal. More bones were still buried in the badlands, waiting to be discovered.

The Bones in the Badlands

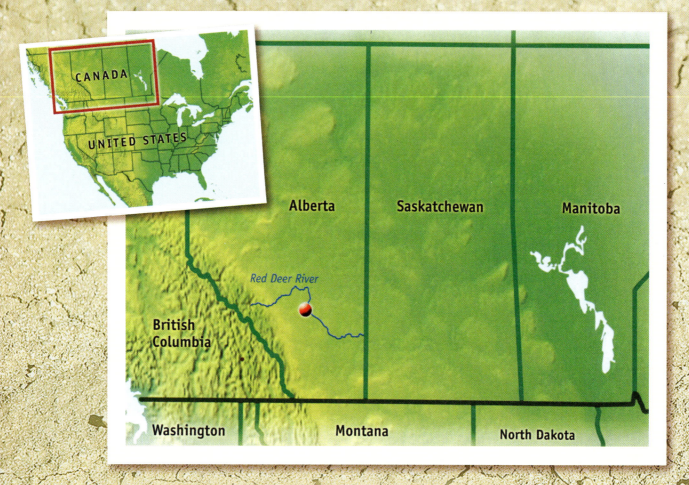

CANADA

UNITED STATES

Alberta

Saskatchewan

Manitoba

Red Deer River

British Columbia

Washington

Montana

North Dakota

Place where Philip rediscovered the *Albertosaurus* fossil site first found by Barnum Brown

Philip discovered more than bones at the museum. He also found Brown's field notes and a photo of Brown's site. Using these clues, Philip was able to find the bone bed.

> ✓ **STOP AND THINK**
>
> **Conclusions** Why did finding so many albertosaur fossils in one place make the team believe that albertosaurs had lived together?

Locating the spot was just the first step, however. Philip and his team worked for months to dig out each fossil. At least 22 albertosaurs were buried in the rock.

After the work was done, a new question came up. Did finding many fossils together **prove** that the animals had lived, died, and even hunted as a group?

Philip uncovering *Albertosaurus* bones in the badlands

In the days of Barnum Brown, fossil hunters were not always able to keep good records. Today, paleontologists carefully record their finds with photographs, drawings, maps, and reports.

What May Have Happened

Philip knew there could be other reasons for the fossils being together. Many of these ideas only brought up more questions, however.

For example, the albertosaurs could have died in quicksand. Yet different kinds of dinosaurs could die in quicksand. Philip had found the fossils of only one kind— *Albertosaurus*.

Maybe the albertosaurs had gathered to lay eggs. If so, however, the fossils should have been about the same age and size. Yet Philip had found small, young animals as well as large, old animals.

Philip's hunt had ended. Yet he needed more evidence to show that the meat-eaters had lived together.

A reconstructed nest of fossilized dinosaur eggs

Scientists know that dinosaurs laid eggs because fossil eggs of several kinds of dinosaurs have been found.

More Groups of Meat-Eaters

Rodolfo Coria uncovers teeth on a huge dinosaur jawbone.

More evidence came when a paleontologist named Rodolfo Coria phoned Philip. Coria was calling from Argentina. He also had found a spot where a group of meat-eating dinosaurs was buried. So perhaps meat-eaters did live in groups after all.

Scientists found more places with groups of meat-eating dinosaurs. These places were all over—Arizona, Montana, South Dakota, Utah, Mongolia, and Zimbabwe.

Philip also looked carefully at the footprints of meat-eating dinosaurs in the Peace River Canyon of Canada. The footprints showed that meat-eating dinosaurs may have traveled together.

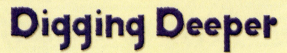

Digging Deeper

Did some meat-eating dinosaurs spend time living and hunting together? Scientists still aren't sure. They can only make smart guesses based on the fossils they have found.

Other questions are still unanswered as well. Why did the albertosaurs at Brown's site die? What killed so many animals at one time? A big storm? A forest fire?

Philip Currie says that a paleontologist is like a detective. The mysterious death happened millions of years ago. No one saw it. Using clues, the scientist tries to tell what happened, how, and why. As long as there are fossils waiting to be found, the investigation continues.

By studying fossils, experts can create models like this life-size *Albertosaurus*.

Your Turn

Questions, Please

Write Your Questions
Many questions about *Albertosaurus* and about other science topics have not yet been answered. What science questions would you like the answer to? Write them. SCIENCE

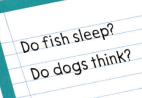

Do fish sleep?
Do dogs think?

Be a Quiz Whiz

Make a Game Work with a group to make a trivia game about *Albertosaurus.* Get several index cards. On one side of each card, write a question about *Albertosaurus* or its discovery. Write the answer on the other side. Then take turns quizzing each other.

SMALL GROUP

Use the Clues

Turn and Talk Authors often let readers draw their own conclusions. With a partner, review the facts about Phillip Currie's search for Brown's bone bed. What conclusions can you draw about the kind of person Phillip Currie is? CONCLUSIONS

✓ TARGET VOCABULARY

fossils	skeletons
clues	uncovering
remains	buried
prove	fierce
evidence	location

GENRE

Informational text gives factual information about a topic. This is a website. After you read, discuss your opinion of fossil hunting. Does it sound interesting? Include details from the article to support your opinion.

TEXT FOCUS

A **chart** is a drawing that lists information in a clear way. Look at the chart on page 61. In which column would you look to find out what to bring on a fossil hunt? How did you know where to look?

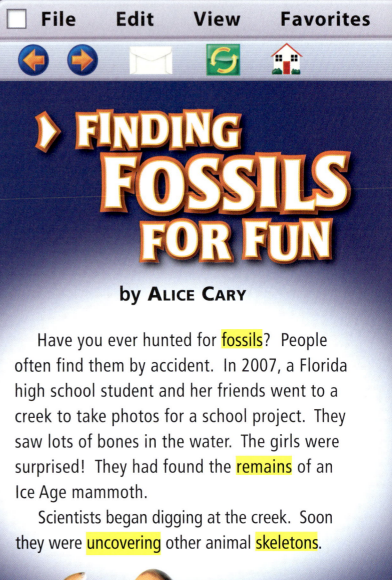

❯ FINDING FOSSILS FOR FUN

by ALICE CARY

Have you ever hunted for fossils? People often find them by accident. In 2007, a Florida high school student and her friends went to a creek to take photos for a school project. They saw lots of bones in the water. The girls were surprised! They had found the remains of an Ice Age mammoth.

Scientists began digging at the creek. Soon they were uncovering other animal skeletons.

A mammoth skeleton gives clues about how a mammoth looked.

Fossils

Fossils are evidence of ancient life. Sometimes dirt or sand covers leaves and bones. Layers of dirt and sand protect these remains from damage. The layers build up as time passes. After many years, the remains harden and become fossils.

You may find fossils buried near you! The chart gives you tips for hunting them.

Hunting Guide

Where to Look	What to Hunt	Tools	Searching Tips
layers of rock	eggs, nests	hammer and chisel	Work carefully so you don't miss anything.
layers of sand or mud	footprints, leaf impressions	notebook, pen, camera	Take notes to keep track of where each discovery was found.
deserts, canyons, cliffs, hills, and mountains	shells	plastic box or newspapers and rubber bands for carrying finds	

Anyone Can Find Fossils!

You're never too young to find fossils. David Shiffler loved <mark>fierce</mark> dinosaurs. In 1995, when he was only three years old, David dug up a green rock. He called it a dinosaur egg.

David's father took the rock to a museum a few months later. David was right! He had found a piece of dinosaur egg! Scientists could <mark>prove</mark> it. The egg was about 150 million years old!

Hunt Fossils Safely

▶ **Take an adult.**
▶ **Choose a safe <mark>location</mark>.**
▶ **Get permission to hunt before you start.**
▶ **Wear safety glasses.**

COOL CLICKS!

Museums with Fossils

Fossils in the News

Fossil Finds

Making Connections

 Text to Self

Be a Fossil Hunter After reading about people who hunt for fossils, do you think you'd like to be a fossil hunter? Write a paragraph explaining why or why not.

 Text to Text

Tell the Steps Work in pairs. Take turns telling the steps to take when you go fossil hunting, based on what you read in *The Albertosaurus Mystery* and "Finding Fossils for Fun." Make sure no steps are left out. Try to tell the steps in the correct order.

 Text to World

Connect to Science Dinosaurs lived on Earth for about 150 million years! Scientists divide this time into the Triassic, Jurassic, and Cretaceous periods. Find out the dates of each of those periods, take notes, and then make a timeline to show what you found.

Pterosaurus

Grammar

Articles

The words *a*, *an*, and *the* are called **articles**. Use *a* and *an* with singular nouns. Use *a* before words that begin with a consonant sound. Use *an* before words that begin with a vowel sound. Use *the* before both singular and plural nouns.

Academic Language

article

Jess found **a** dinosaur bone.

He searched in **an** old cave.

I saw **the** bone yesterday.

The scientists at the museum want to see it, too.

Turn and Talk   **Work with a partner. Read each group of words aloud. Decide which article may be used before each word.**

1 (a, an) egg

2 (the, an) kite

3 (a, an) red hat

4 (the, an) bumpy road

5 (a, an) hour

6 (a, an) angry bull

Word Choice Adjectives add details about people, places, and things. When you write, use exact adjectives so your reader can better picture what you are saying.

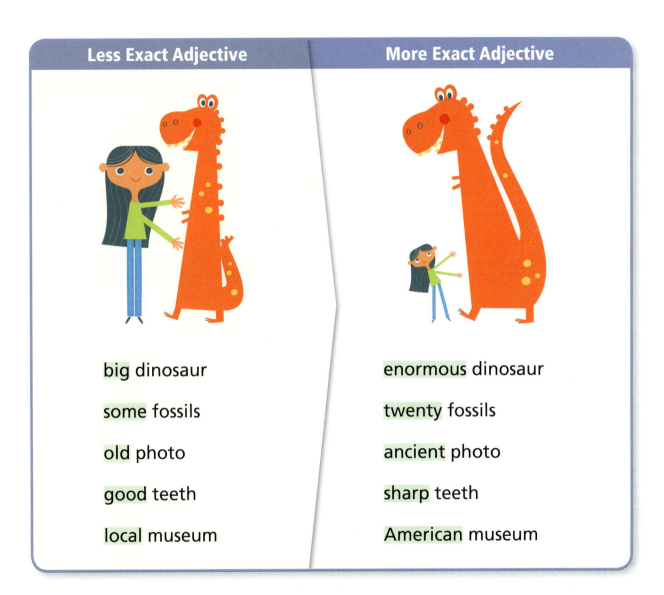

Less Exact Adjective	More Exact Adjective
big dinosaur	**enormous** dinosaur
some fossils	**twenty** fossils
old photo	**ancient** photo
good teeth	**sharp** teeth
local museum	**American** museum

Connect Grammar to Writing

As you revise your opinion paragraph, try to use exact adjectives.

Write to Persuade

The author of *The Albertosaurus Mystery* thinks fossil hunting is exciting. By sharing what really interests her, she gets her readers excited too. In your **opinion** paragraph, add ideas and details that will make your readers say, "Wow! I see what you mean!"

Rick wrote his opinion of studying prehistoric people. Later, he added more details to support his opinion.

Writing Traits Checklist

✓ **Ideas**
Did I explain my ideas clearly?

✓ **Organization**
Did I begin by telling my opinion?

✓ **Word Choice**
Did I use exact adjectives?

✓ **Voice**
Are my supporting reasons and details right for my audience?

✓ **Sentence Fluency**
Do my sentences flow smoothly?

✓ **Conventions**
Did I punctuate my sentences correctly?

Revised Draft

I love learning about prehistoric people. The way scientists study them is ~~interesting~~. like solving a mysterious puzzle. Prehistoric people left no books about their lives. They just left objects that give clues. I am also amazed by how they got along without modern inventions. They lived in caves or huts, even in freezing weather. Imagine camping out for your whole life!

Amazing People from the Past
by Rick Yoshida

I love learning about prehistoric people. The way scientists study them is like solving a mysterious puzzle. Prehistoric people left no books about their lives. They just left objects that give clues. I am also amazed by how they got along without modern inventions. They lived in caves or huts, even in freezing weather. Imagine camping out for your whole life! They got all their food by hunting or finding plants. Don't you wonder what kids did for fun? There are lots of great facts to learn about prehistoric people.

> I added details that will make my opinion clear. I also used exact adjectives.

Reading as a Writer

What reasons support Rick's opinion best? Where can you add more persuasive details in your own paper?

Poems about Nature

A TREE IS GROWING

pollen

store

clumps

passages

absorb

throughout

coverings

spines

tropical

dissolve

Vocabulary Reader

Context Cards

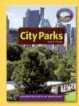

City Parks

Vocabulary in Context

1 pollen

This bee carries **pollen** from flower to flower, which helps seeds grow.

2 store

A baobab tree can **store**, or keep, lots of water in its trunk.

3 clumps

The flowers on some trees grow in **clumps**, or bunches.

4 passages

A leaf has small **passages**, or tubes, that allow water to spread all over.

- Study each **Context Card**.
- Make up a new context sentence using two Vocabulary words.

5 absorb

A plant's roots **absorb** water. They soak it up.

6 throughout

Sap passes **throughout** a tree. It travels to every part.

7 coverings

Different kinds of trees have different **coverings**, or outer layers.

8 spines

Many kinds of cacti are covered in sharp **spines**.

9 tropical

Some plants grow in warm, damp, **tropical** climates near the equator.

10 dissolve

If you add salt to water, it will **dissolve**, or mix, with the water.

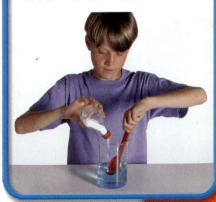

Background

Tree Talk All trees have roots that **absorb** water. Minerals **dissolve** in that water. The water and minerals then travel through **passages** in the trunk. Some trees in dry climates have special trunks that help them **store** water. When a tree needs a drink, the stored water spreads **throughout** the branches. **Tropical** rain forests do not have this problem. Rain there is so plentiful, trees and giant **clumps** of green plants rarely go thirsty!

Trees have many different kinds of **coverings**. Some have **spines** for protection. Others have thick bark. Some trees have flowers, which produce **pollen**.

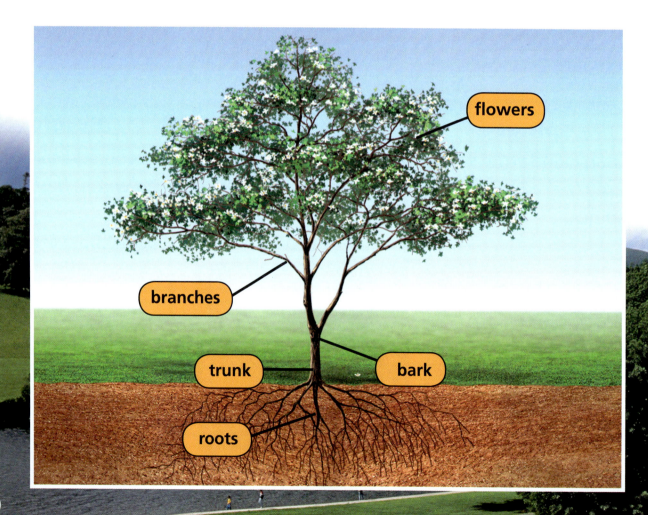

flowers

branches

trunk

bark

roots

Comprehension

Text and Graphic Features

The author of *A Tree Is Growing* uses text and graphic features to make ideas about trees clear. Use a chart like this to list some features and the purpose of each feature.

Text or Graphic Feature	Page	Purpose

Question

When you have a question or are confused about what you are reading, look for pictures, diagrams, or charts that show what the text describes. Ask yourself, *How can this text or graphic feature help me better understand what I am reading?*

A TREE IS GROWING

✓ TARGET VOCABULARY

pollen	throughout
store	coverings
clumps	spines
passages	tropical
absorb	dissolve

 ### ✓ TARGET SKILL

Text and Graphic Features Tell how words and art work together.

✓ TARGET STRATEGY

Question Ask and answer questions before you read, while you read, and after you read to stay more focused on the text.

GENRE

Informational text gives factual information about a topic.

MEET THE AUTHOR
Arthur Dorros

Arthur Dorros loves trees. When he was five, he planted a maple seedling. The tree grew taller than a two-story house! The author believes that everyone has stories to tell. He encourages children all over the country to write.

MEET THE ILLUSTRATOR
S. D. Schindler

When S. D. Schindler was just four years old, he won a red wagon in a coloring contest. S. D. Schindler loves nature as much as he loves art. He used plants and animals from the woods near his home as models for the illustrations in *A Tree Is Growing*.

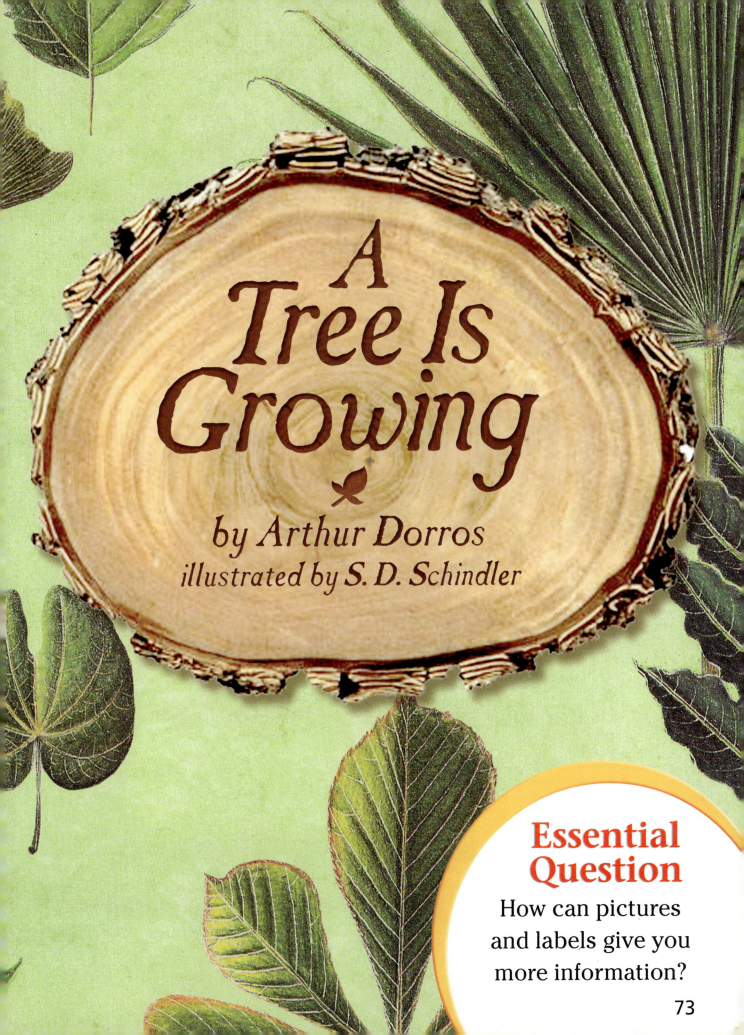

A Tree Is Growing

by Arthur Dorros
illustrated by S. D. Schindler

Essential Question

How can pictures and labels give you more information?

A giant tree may look as if it has always been big. But even the biggest tree keeps growing and changing.

In the spring you can see that a tree is growing as you watch buds on the branches unfold into leaves.

Bristlecone pines are the oldest known living trees on earth. Some have been growing for five thousand years—since before the pyramids in Egypt were built.

White oak

Palm

Gingko

Leaves can be skinny needles or big heart shapes. Whatever shape or size a leaf is, it makes food for the tree.

A kind of sugar is made in the leaves. Trees use the sugar as food.

Breadfruit tree

Empress tree

White pine

Red maple

76

*If you rub a
sassafras leaf,
the sap smells spicy.*

The sugary water made in the leaves is mixed with other tree juices called sap. The food in the sap is carried throughout the tree. Where a branch breaks or where bark is cut, sap oozes out of a tree. The strong smells of some saps can keep insects from eating the trees they live on.

*Maple syrup is the
boiled sap of sugar
maple trees.*

Moth
caterpillar

Baobab trees *store*
water in the trunks.
When a baobab tree
trunk is swollen with
water, it is round and
fat. In dry weather,
the tree gets water
from the trunk. Then
the trunk gets thinner.

78

Water

A tree needs sunlight, air, soil, and water to grow.

Water travels through <mark>passages</mark> in the trunk and branches up to the leaves. The water moves up the trunk as if it is being sucked through a straw.

Sugary sap made in the leaves travels down other passages in the trunk, taking food to different parts of the tree.

STOP AND THINK

Question What is shown in the diagram? Use the information in paragraph 2 to help you understand what is happening.

A few kinds of trees drop roots from branches into the soil to gather water. Banyan tree roots grow into columns all around the tree.

Growing roots are strong. A root can lift a sidewalk or split a rock as it grows. By splitting the rock, it helps make soil.

White oak

Earthworms

Beetle grub

The roots of a tree grow into the ground and hold the tree in place. Roots are like pipelines. They ==absorb== water and carry it into the tree.

A tree's roots spread out far underground. They usually grow out a little farther than the tree's branches.

Trees need minerals to grow. Minerals are tiny particles that are found in the soil. Salt is one kind of mineral. Like salt, other minerals ==dissolve== in water. They are mixed in with the water that roots absorb and are carried throughout the tree.

Mushrooms growing among the roots of a tree can help it get minerals. And the mushrooms and plants growing near a tree get water brought by the tree's roots.

Bicolored boletus mushrooms

Flicker

Bark is the skin of a tree. The outer layer of bark protects the tree. When an oak tree is young, the bark is as smooth as a baby's skin. As the tree grows older, the bark becomes rough and cracked.

STOP AND THINK

Author's Craft How does the author help readers picture what oak tree bark is like when it is young and when it is old?

Polyphemus moth

Looking at the bark of a tree can help you know what kind of tree it is.

The cork used for bulletin boards is the peeled-off outer bark of a cork oak tree.

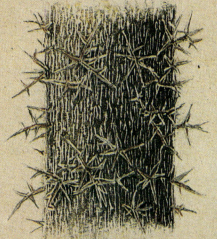

Honey locust bark has spines to help protect the tree.

In cool climates, cambium only grows in spring and summer. Count growth rings to see how old a tree was when it died. An old fir tree can have over a thousand rings, one for each year it lived.

In *tropical* rain forest trees, the cambium grows all year and there are no rings. It is hard to tell the ages of those trees.

Growth rings

Snail

Phloem

Cambium

Xylem

✔ **STOP AND THINK**

Text and Graphic Features How do the captions, labels, and diagrams help you understand the selection?

Underwing moth

The bark you can touch and see is not growing anymore. Underneath it is a layer of growing bark, called *cambium*. Each year's cambium growth is a ring in the wood of a tree. As trees add new cambium, the trees become bigger around.

Next to the cambium are two layers called *xylem* and *phloem*. Water from the roots moves through the xylem, and sap from the leaves moves through the phloem.

Trees grow bigger around, and they grow taller. As a tree grows, lower branches may fall off, making the trunk look longer. But the branches do not move upward on the trunk. A tree grows taller only at the top, as the tips of the top branches grow upward.

If you find a mark on a tree trunk today, that mark would stay at the same height for as long as the tree lives.

10 years

20 years

30 years

Wild turkey

50 years   200 years

Sequoias are some of the tallest trees in the world—over three hundred feet tall.

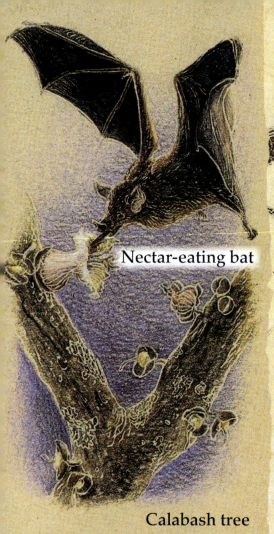

Nectar-eating bat

Calabash tree

Catkins

Purple finch
(male)

Saucer
magnolia

Birds, insects, and even bats are attracted to flowers to drink their sweet juices. When they brush the flowers, the animals get a powder called ==pollen== on them. The animals carry the pollen to other flowers. When the pollen mixes with certain parts of the flowers, seeds grow. Wind also helps pollinate flowers.

In the spring, you can smell tree flowers. Tree flowers are found in many shapes and colors, and have many different smells. Parts of the flowers grow to become seeds. Oak trees have dangling clumps of flowers called catkins that help make acorns, the seeds of an oak tree.

Honey bee

Wild cherry

Purple finch
(female)

Sugar maple

An oak tree can drop more than fifty thousand acorns in one year. Only a few of them grow into oak trees. Most are eaten, are crushed, rot, or land in a place where they cannot take root.

Acorns can be carried away and dropped or buried by animals to grow in new places. Other kinds of seeds blow in the wind or float on water.

Sugar maple seed

Acorns

Gray
squirrel

Different kinds of trees
make seeds with
different ==coverings==.
Nuts, cones, and fruits
all have seeds inside.

Brazil nut

Mountain
pine cone

Cherry

Coconuts are seeds of
a palm tree. A coconut
can float across the
ocean and sprout on a
sandy beach.

91

In cool climates, trees stop growing in autumn. The leaves of many trees stop making sugary food for the tree, and they lose their green color. Then you can see the red, brown, yellow, and orange colors that are also in the leaves.

Pine trees and some other trees have needles or leaves that do not change color in autumn.

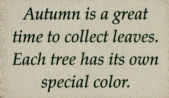

Tulip poplar

Gingko

Big-tooth aspen

Sweet gum

Pin oak

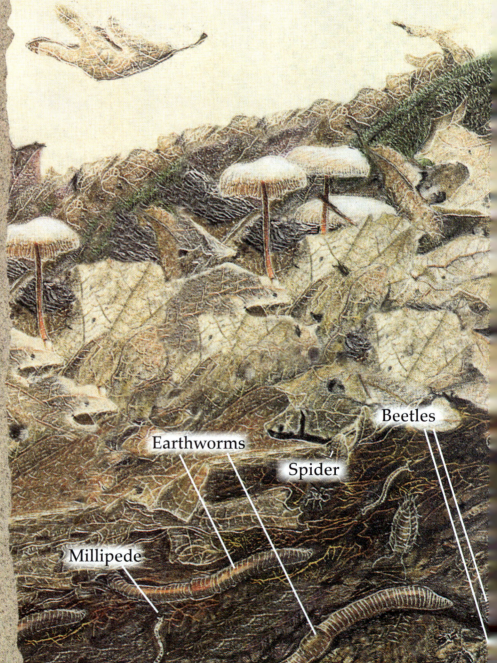

Beetles

Earthworms

Spider

Millipede

Mole

When leaves fall to the ground, insects and
worms eat them. The chewed and eaten bits
of leaves make the soil better for growing trees
and other plants.

Trees rest in the cold of winter, and their branches are bare. They may look as if they are dead. But look closely and you can see small buds that will become leaves and flowers in the spring.

In the spring, listen to the wind rustling the leaves. The trees are growing again.

White oak

White oak

Horse chestnut

Your Turn

Picture It

Write Labels What kinds of trees grow where you live? Draw a picture of a tree near your home or school. Then use information you learned from the selection to write labels for your tree. SCIENCE

needles

cone

trunk

Tree Talk

Conduct an Interview Imagine that a tree could talk. What might it say? Work with a partner. Role-play a radio interview with a tree. One of you should take the part of the tree. The other should be the interviewer. The interviewer should ask the tree questions, such as how it grew, what it needs to survive, and what it likes and doesn't like. PARTNERS

A Picture's Worth 1,000 Words

Turn and Talk With a partner, look back through the selection. Discuss the kinds of extra information the pictures and labels add. How do the pictures and labels help you better understand the text?

TEXT AND GRAPHIC FEATURES

Poetry

✓ **TARGET VOCABULARY**

pollen	throughout
store	coverings
clumps	spines
passages	tropical
absorb	dissolve

GENRE

Poetry uses the sound and rhythm of words to show images and express feelings.

TEXT FOCUS

Personification gives human traits to objects, animals, and plants. Discuss which human characteristics are given to the sea and the mountains in these two poems. Say which words make them look, feel, and sound like people.

Poems About Nature

The poems you will read next are about nature. What is the mood, or feeling, of each poem? Which words or rhythms help create this mood?

Until I Saw the Sea

Until I saw the sea
I did not know
that wind
could wrinkle water so.

I never knew
that sun
could splinter a whole sea of blue.

Nor
did I know before,
a sea breathes in and out
upon a shore.

by Lilian Moore

Fog coverings may hide a mountaintop completely. The mountain appears to dissolve into the gray mist.

Mountain Mist

tender
breath
of mountains

playful
steam
clouding

the windows
of the village
bakery

the golden
eyeglasses
of my father

the windshield
of my family's
station wagon

as we cross
Mexico's western
mountain range

by Francisco X. Alarcón

From high to low tide, the ocean's depth can change by up to fifty feet! As the tide goes down, the water carves narrow passages in the sand.

97

Knockabout and Knockaboom

Mohave Desert
Southwestern United States

The wind that whistles desert songs
    By spinning tops of sand
Leaves behind a silent sea
    Of dune-upon-dune land.

The Land of Sand turns hot as fire,
    But once or twice a year
Into the picture of a sky
    Two thunderclouds appear.

They knockabout and knockaboom
    To make a THUNDERSHOWER!
And when they leave, they always leave
    At least . . . one desert flower.

by J. Patrick Lewis

Like other deserts throughout the world, the Mojave Desert is dry. When rain falls, desert plants absorb as much water as they can. A large saguaro cactus can store nearly a ton of water in its spines! If spring brings enough rainfall, clumps of bright flowers appear. Bees buzz from blossom to blossom, collecting pollen. For a short while, the desert looks almost lush and tropical!

Write a Nature Poem

Write your own nature poem. Try including personification.

Making Connections

 Text to Self

A Tree and Me In what ways are you like a tree? In what ways are you different? Work in a small group. Take turns telling things you have in common with a tree, and ways you are different.

 Text to Text

Write a Poem Choose your favorite poem from "Poems About Nature." Then write your own poem in a similar style about a tree included in *A Tree Is Growing*. Use words that help the reader see, hear, smell, and feel the tree.

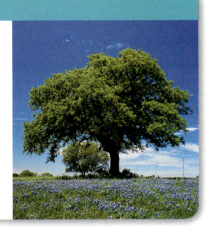

 Text to World

Connect to Science Research a local tree at the library. Inspect this type of tree in person. Take notes about the tree. Write a paragraph that gives important facts about the tree. Then draw a picture to go with your paragraph.

Grammar

Using the Verb *be* and Helping Verbs The verbs *am*, *is*, *was*, *are*, and *were* are forms of the verb *be*. They do not show action. They tell what someone or something is or was.

Subject	Present	Past
I	am	was
you	are	were
he, she, it	is	was
singular noun *(Thomas)*	is	was
plural noun *(trees)*, we, they	are	were

Sometimes the words *has* and *have* help other verbs to show past time. *Has* and *have* are called **helping verbs**.

Subject	Helping Verb
he, she, it	He **has** watched the trees grow.
I, you, we, they	They **have** grown very tall.

 **Write each sentence correctly using the verb that best completes each sentence.**

1 I (is, am) a great tree climber.

2 The girls (has, have) picked apples.

3 They (was, were) at the orchard yesterday.

100

Sentence Fluency When two sentences have the same predicate, you can put the sentences together. Join the two subjects and use the word *and* between them. You may have to change the forms of the verbs *be* and *have* to go with their subjects.

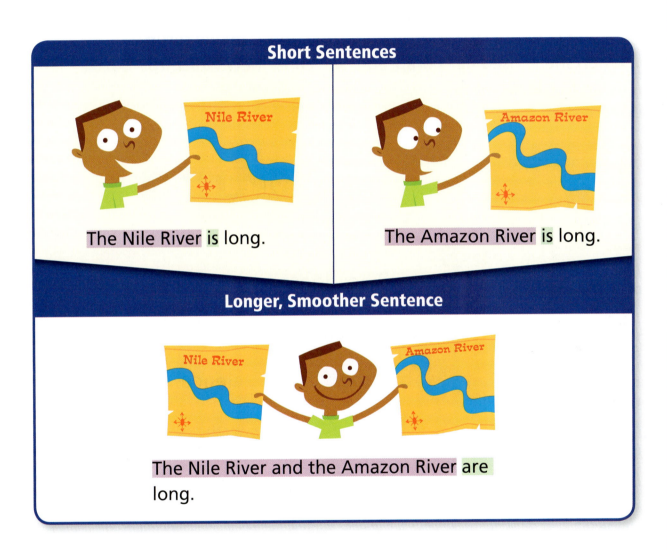

Short Sentences

The Nile River is long.

The Amazon River is long.

Longer, Smoother Sentence

The Nile River and the Amazon River are long.

Connect Grammar to Writing

As you revise your persuasive essay, try to combine subjects to make longer sentences. Change the verb form to make it go with the subject.

Write to Persuade

✔ **Word Choice** In *A Tree Is Growing*, the author writes that tree bark "becomes rough and cracked." As you revise your **problem and solution paragraph**, try to use exact words, too.

Tanya wrote to a science magazine about maple syrup. When she revised her paragraph, she chose new words to make her ideas clear.

Writing Traits Checklist

✔ **Ideas**
Did I use supporting ideas and examples?

✔ **Organization**
Did I clearly state the problem and solution?

✔ **Word Choice**
Did I use clear, exact words?

✔ **Voice**
Do I sound sure of my ideas?

✔ **Sentence Fluency**
Did I use both simple and compound sentences?

✔ **Conventions**
Did I write neatly in cursive script?

Revised Draft

Who doesn't love maple syrup? It's great on ~~food~~ waffles and pancakes. It also would be ~~good~~ an interesting subject for a science article. I am sure people would ~~like~~ enjoy reading about it.

102

The Next Science Article

by Tanya Petrov

Who doesn't love maple syrup? It's great on waffles and pancakes. It also would be an interesting subject for a science article. I am sure people would enjoy reading about it.

Maple syrup is made from the sap of sugar maple trees. The article could tell about the journey from inside the tree to inside the refrigerator. It could also tell how people discovered maple syrup and how they made it in the past. Both students and scientists could learn about this natural treat.

> I added some exact words. I also combined two sentences to avoid repeating a predicate.

Reading as a Writer

Why did Tanya replace "food" with "waffles and pancakes"? Where can you add more exact words in your own paper?

103

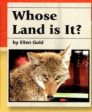

fiery

within

horrifying

ancient

mysterious

emergency

panicking

scientific

prehistoric

immediately

Vocabulary Reader | Context Cards

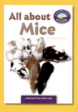

Vocabulary in Context

1 fiery

After this **fiery** building has cooled, rescue dogs may go inside to help.

2 within

Within seconds, this helper dog finds and pushes the right button.

3 horrifying

This dog is used to the deep snow. He does not find it **horrifying**, or scary.

4 ancient

Ancient art from Roman times proves people kept dogs as pets long ago.

● Study each **Context Card**.

● Tell a story about two or more pictures, using Vocabulary words.

5 mysterious

This dog is sniffing at a <mark>mysterious</mark> package to help guess what it holds.

6 emergency

A rescue dog can help an <mark>emergency</mark> team find trapped people quickly.

7 panicking

Herding dogs can help guide scared, or <mark>panicking</mark>, animals.

8 scientific

People do <mark>scientific</mark> research to create new medicines that can help sick dogs.

9 prehistoric

Dogs helped people hunt in <mark>prehistoric</mark> times, which were very long ago.

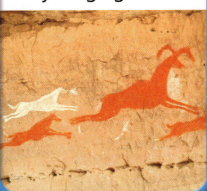

10 immediately

As soon as the light changes, this dog <mark>immediately</mark> walks forward.

Background

The Power of Volcanoes People have lived with volcanoes since ==prehistoric== times. ==Ancient== cultures found volcanoes ==mysterious==. They thought they were alive! When ==fiery== lava ==within== the volcano erupted, people thought the volcano was angry. It was ==horrifying==!

Today, ==scientific== facts explain why volcanoes erupt. Active volcanoes are checked daily. A warning is given before an eruption can cause an ==emergency== situation. People can leave the area ==immediately== without ==panicking==, and lives are saved.

Scientists are careful when they study lava, which is nearly 2000 degrees! When lava cools, it hardens into rock. That's how the Hawaiian Islands formed.

Comprehension

Cause and Effect

In *Dogzilla*, some events cause other events to happen. The first event is the cause. The second event is the effect. Use a chart like this one to identify causes and effects as you read.

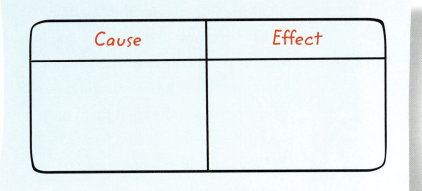

Cause	Effect

✔ **TARGET STRATEGY** **Summarize**

You can use the causes and effects from your chart to summarize, or retell, the most important events in *Dogzilla*. This will help you understand what you read.

TARGET VOCABULARY

fiery	emergency
within	panicking
horrifying	scientific
ancient	prehistoric
mysterious	immediately

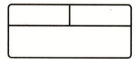

TARGET SKILL

Cause and Effect Tell how one event makes another happen and why.

TARGET STRATEGY

Summarize Tell the important parts of the story in your own words.

GENRE

A **fantasy** is a story that could not happen in real life. Use what you know about the genre to set a purpose for reading.

MEET THE AUTHOR AND ILLUSTRATOR

Dav Pilkey

Warning: *Dogzilla* is rated EG for "Extremely Goofy." Ever since he was eight years old, Dav Pilkey has been making extremely goofy books.
To create illustrations for *Dogzilla*, Pilkey first took photos of his dog Leia and his pet mice Flash, Rabies, and Dwayne. Then he cut the animals out of the photos and pasted them onto backgrounds that he had painted.
By the way, Pilkey's first name is pronounced just like Dave.

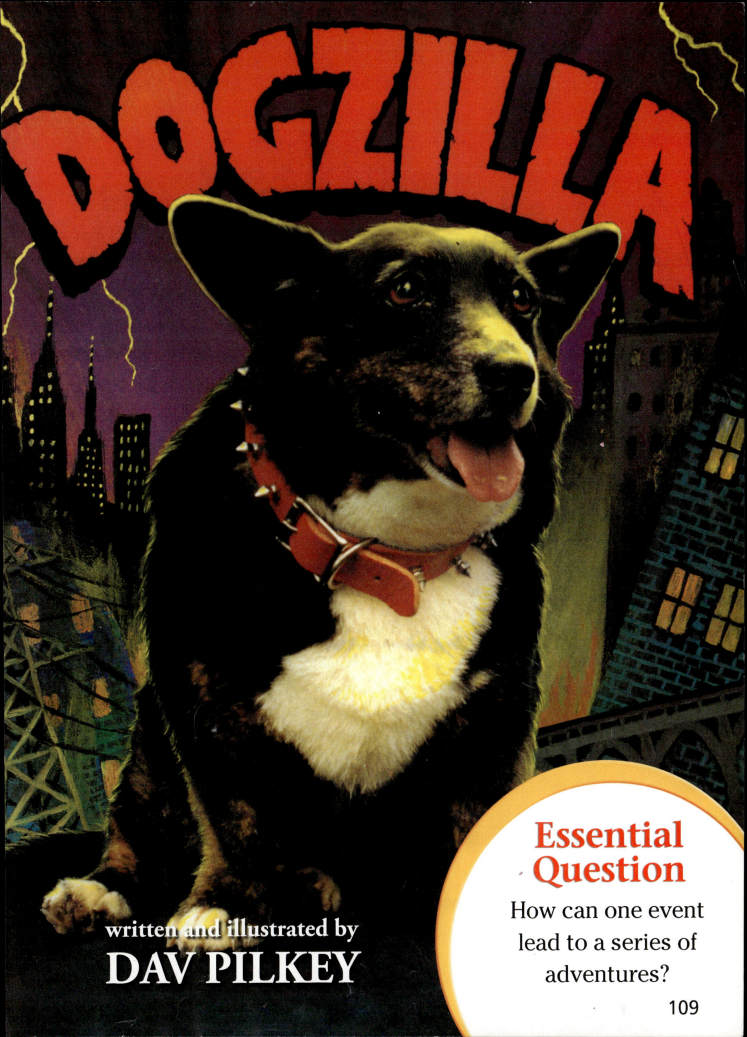

DOGZILLA

written and illustrated by
DAV PILKEY

Essential Question

How can one event lead to a series of adventures?

It was summertime in the city of Mousopolis,

and mice from all corners of the community had come together to compete in the First Annual Barbecue Cook-Off.

As the cook-off got under way, smoke from the hot grills lifted the irresistible scent of barbecue sauce over the rooftops of the city.

A gentle wind carried the mouth-watering smell into the distance, right over the top of an ancient crater. Before long, a strange and <mark>mysterious</mark> sound was heard: "Sniff . . . sniff. Sniff . . . sniff sniff sniff sniff . . ."

All at once, the volcano began to tremble.
And suddenly, up from the very depths of the earth came the most terrifying creature ever known to mousekind: the dreadful Dogzilla!

 **STOP AND THINK**

Cause and Effect What events take place that cause Dogzilla to come out of the volcano? What do you predict will happen next?

, soldiers were sent out to stop the mighty beast. The heroic troops were led by their brave commanding officer, the Big Cheese.

"All right, you old fleabag," squeaked the Big Cheese, "get those paws in the air—you're coming with us!"

116

Without warning, the monstrous mutt breathed her horrible breath onto the mice.

"Doggy breath!" screamed the soldiers. "Run for your lives!"

"Hey, come back here," shouted the Big Cheese to his troops. "What are you, men or mice?"

"We're MICE," they squeaked.

"Hmmmm," said the Big Cheese, "you're *right*! . . . Wait for me!"

The colossal canine followed the soldiers back to
Mousopolis, licking up all of the food in her path.
Afterward, Dogzilla wandered through the city
streets, doing those things that come naturally to dogs.
Dogzilla chased cars—right off the freeway!

Dogzilla chewed furniture—and the furniture store as well.
And Dogzilla dug up bones—at the Museum of Natural
History.

Meanwhile, the Big Cheese had organized an emergency meeting with one of the city's greatest scientific minds, Professor Scarlett O'Hairy.

"Gentlemice," said Professor O'Hairy, "this monster comes from prehistoric times. It is perhaps millions of years old."

"Maybe we could teach it to do something positive for the community," suggested the Big Cheese.

"I'm afraid not," said Professor O'Hairy. "You simply can't teach an old dog new tricks!

"If we're going to defeat this dog, we've got to *think* like a dog! We've got to find something that *all* dogs are afraid of—something that will scare this beast away from Mousopolis FOREVER!"

"I've got an idea," squeaked the Big Cheese . . .

STOP AND THINK

Author's Craft Which details does the author use in the words and pictures to make the mice seem like people?

Within minutes, the mice had assembled at the center of town.

"All right, Dogzilla," shouted the Big Cheese, "no more Mister Mice Guy—it's BATHTIME!"

Suddenly, a blast of warm, sudsy water hit Dogzilla with tremendous force.

The panicking pooch let out a burst of hot, fiery breath, and the chase was on!

The Big Cheese tried to catch up to the hot dog with all the relish he could muster.

Dogzilla hightailed it out of town, and back into the mouth of the ==ancient== volcano.

"Well, I'll be dog-goned," squeaked the Big Cheese. "It worked!"

With the ==horrifying== memory of the bubble bath etched in her mind forever, Dogzilla never again returned to Mousopolis.

STOP AND THINK

Summarize Summarize the ways in which Big Cheese and his troops respond to Dogzilla's attack on Mousopolis.

Within a year, Mousopolis had rebuilt itself . . . just in time for the Second Annual Barbecue Cook-Off. The mice of Mousopolis fired up their grills, confident that they would never see or hear from Dogzilla again.

However, there was one thing they hadn't counted on . . .

Puppies!

Your Turn

Rate It!

Book Review On a scale of 1 to 10, with 10 being the best, what score would you give *Dogzilla*? What did you like or not like about the story? Write a short book review. Tell readers whether they should read the story.

PERSONAL RESPONSE

Dogzilla

Picture a Story

Make a Collage With a partner, cut out pictures from old magazines of different animals and places. Paste the pictures on a big piece of paper to make a collage like the ones in *Dogzilla*. Then make up a story about the animal characters in your collage.

PARTNERS

One Thing Leads to Another

Turn and Talk In *Dogzilla,* the smell of barbecue begins a chain of events. With a partner, discuss why the Big Cheese has to call an emergency meeting. What happens as a result of the meeting? Then think about the story's ending. What troubles might the puppies cause?

CAUSE AND EFFECT

TODAY'S

Monday, September 5, 2010

Whose Land Is It?

by Ellen Gold

People and Wild Animals

People and animals need places to live. Animals have lived in the wilderness for thousands of years. They live in ==ancient== forests, oceans, and other habitats. Yet wild animals also live in people's yards. They live in cities, too!

Coyotes are no strangers to cities. One even walked into a restaurant in Chicago! ==Within== moments, a ==panicking== worker had climbed onto the counter.

NEWS

Community	**Classifieds**
Third Graders	Looking for a
Meet the Mayor	new pet?

FROM THE PAGES OF
WEEKLY READER

Running into an unexpected alligator can be **horrifying**. People may have to take **emergency** steps, like having a trapper catch the animal.

Habitat Loss

Why are wild animals moving closer to people? They are losing their habitats. Then they must find new places to live.

Fires destroy many animals' homes. Some years are especially **fiery**. In 2006, fires burned nearly 10 million acres of wild land in the United States.

People destroy habitats, too. People build homes, stores, and roads where wild animals live. In Florida many homes are near swamps and waterways. These are places where alligators live.

Continued from page 129

Changing Ways

Alligators have been around since ==prehistoric== times. They mostly fear people. Yet that may be changing. Why is this?

The reason is far from ==mysterious==. Some people feed alligators. Then those alligators stop fearing people. They may think that all people will feed them.

Other animals link people to food, too. ==Scientific== experts know a lot about black bears. Country bears look for food during the day. City bears eat at night. They know that people put out garbage. So, city bears find food in dumpsters and trashcans.

How can people keep bears away? People need to change their habits. They should use bear-proof trashcans. They should fasten the cans ==immediately== after use. If bears can't get food, they won't come back.

This black bear has wandered into someone's backyard garden, right in the heart of a big city! Have wild animals ever visited your home?

Making Connections

 Text to Self

Connect to Art Think about a time you had a funny, scary, or interesting experience with an animal. Draw a picture to show what happened.

 Text to Text

People and Animals In *Dogzilla*, the dog is the scary creature who causes danger to the mice. In "Whose Land Is It?," both animals and people cause danger to each other. How? With a partner, discuss how both animals and people can seem scary to each other.

 Text to World

Connect to Science *Dogzilla* is a funny story about a dog, but "Whose Land Is It?" explains that where animals live is a serious issue. Write an essay to convince the reader that people should live cooperatively with wild animals. Include details from the text to support your point.

Grammar

Irregular Verbs Some verbs have a special spelling to show past time. They have another spelling when used with *has, have,* or *had*.

Present	Past	with *has, have,* or *had*
go	went	has, have, had gone
see	saw	has, have, had seen
do	did	has, have, had done
run	ran	has, have, had run
come	came	has, have, had come

 **Work with a partner. Read the sentences aloud. Choose the correct verb for each sentence.**

❶ The dog (come, came) to Mousetown for food.

❷ He had (saw, seen) a barbeque.

❸ He ate everything there, and now he has (ran, run) away.

❹ The mice have (came, come) together to talk.

❺ The mice (did, done) not know what to do!

132

Word Choice When you write, it is important to use exact verbs. Your readers will understand your writing better.

Less Exact Verb	Exact Verb
The mice **ran** away from the giant dog.	The mice **dashed** away from the giant dog. The mice **darted** away from the giant dog. The mice **scampered** away from the giant dog.

Connect Grammar to Writing

As you revise your persuasive essay next week, look for places where you can use exact verbs.

Write to Persuade

☑️ **Ideas** When you plan a **persuasive essay**, picture your audience asking, "Why should I do what you want?" Draw a cartoon to explore your reasons. Later, you can organize your ideas in a persuasion chart.

Daniel wanted to persuade children to join a club. He explored his reasons in the cartoon below. Then he organized his ideas in a chart.

Writing Process Checklist

▶ **Prewrite**

☑️ **Did I think about my purpose?**

☑️ **Did I choose a goal I really care about?**

☑️ **Did I make my position clear?**

☑️ **Did I give reasons that will persuade my audience?**

☑️ **Did I order my reasons?**

Draft

Revise

Edit

Publish and Share

Exploring a Topic

Why should I join the Penguin Club?

It's fun and interesting!

Penguins need help.

You meet new people.

~~Some kids have quit.~~

Persuasion Chart

My Goal: Children should join the Penguin Club.

Reason: It's fun and interesting!

Details: learn cool facts
go to Science Museum
live penguins at the Aquarium

Reason: Penguins need help.

Details: fewer places to live
dogs hunt penguins
oil spills

Reason: You'll meet new people.

Details: kids are nice and love animals
meet our leader, Mr. Spears

I picked my best reasons and chose an order for them. Then I added details.

Reading as a Writer

Which details would persuade you to join Daniel's club? What details can you add to your own chart to persuade your readers?

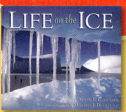

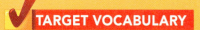
✓ TARGET VOCABULARY

shelter

colony

constant

wilderness

climate

region

unexpected

gliding

overheated

layer

Vocabulary
Reader

Context
Cards

Vocabulary in Context

1 shelter
A tent can make a good **shelter** for an explorer. It is a good place to keep warm.

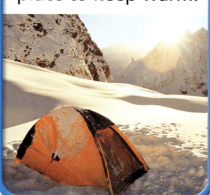

2 colony
Some people take trips to study a **colony**, or large group, of penguins.

3 constant
Steady, or **constant**, rain can make hiking trails slippery and difficult to use.

4 wilderness
Explorers often travel through **wilderness**, or unsettled areas.

- **Study each Context Card.**
- **Place the Vocabulary words in alphabetical order.**

5 climate

Boaters must avoid ice when exploring regions with a very cold climate.

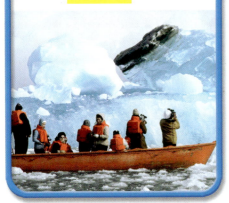

6 region

This overgrown jungle is in a hot and rainy region, or area.

7 unexpected

The view from the top surprised these hikers. It was quite unexpected.

8 gliding

Gliding along, or flying by wind power, is an exciting way to explore.

9 overheated

Smart explorers find shade and drink water when they feel overheated.

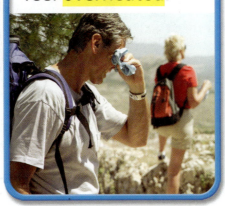

10 layer

A layer of ice must be several inches thick before it is safe to cross.

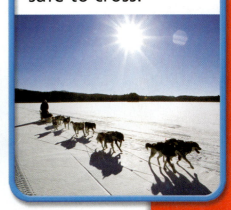

Background

✔ **Life in Antarctica** Would you like to visit the bottom of the world? The region around the South Pole in Antarctica is a frozen, empty wilderness. However, scientists from around the world live and work there in a busy colony. They study the Earth's climate.

Temperatures can sink to –100°F, so scientists must be careful outside the warmth of their shelter. Gliding on skis over a thick layer of snow and ice, they watch for unexpected, deep cracks. One thing is certain here, though. They're unlikely to get overheated!

For half of the year, sunlight at this South Pole base is constant, or always shining. For the other half, it is dark. This time of extra daylight is called the "midnight sun."

Bow of icebreaker in ice in McMurdo Sound with Adélie Penguins (*pygoscelis adeliae*) walking by

Comprehension

Main Ideas and Details

The author of *Life on the Ice* gives important information, or main ideas, about Antarctica. Details in the text help make each main idea clear. As you read, use a chart like this one to show how the details support the main ideas.

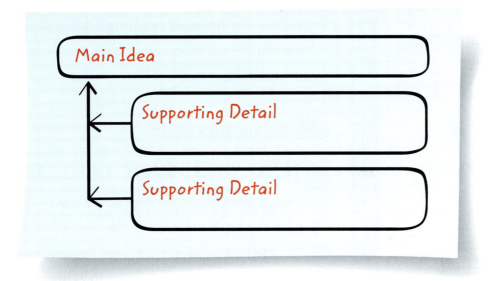

Infer/Predict

Think about the main ideas and details on your chart. Use them to infer, or figure out, more about living and working in Antarctica.

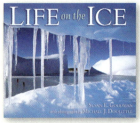

LIFE on the ICE

SUSAN E. GOODMAN
with photographs by MICHAEL J. DOOLITTLE

✔ **TARGET VOCABULARY**

shelter	region
colony	unexpected
constant	gliding
wilderness	overheated
climate	layer

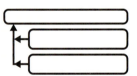

✔ **TARGET SKILL**

Main Ideas and Details
Tell important ideas and details about a topic.

✔ **TARGET STRATEGY**

Infer/Predict Use clues to figure out more about the selection.

GENRE

Informational text gives factual information about a topic. Skim *Life on the Ice* before you read and predict what it will be about.

MEET THE AUTHOR

SUSAN E. GOODMAN

Susan Goodman's life as a writer has taken her on some exciting adventures. She has gone swimming with dolphins in Florida, made friends with animals in the Amazon rain forest, ridden roller coasters in Pennsylvania, and stayed overnight in an underwater hotel.

MEET THE PHOTOGRAPHER

MICHAEL J. DOOLITTLE

To capture the photos for *Life on the Ice*, Michael Doolittle traveled to the Arctic Circle. He had to keep his camera inside his heavy coat to prevent it from freezing. Doolittle has collaborated with Susan Goodman on many books, including the whole *Ultimate Field Trip* series.

LIFE on the ICE

by SUSAN E. GOODMAN
with photographs by MICHAEL J. DOOLITTLE

Essential Question

Where are main ideas often found in nonfiction text?

The top and the bottom of our planet are covered with ice. The top, the Arctic, is home to the North Pole. It can be so cold that a cup of hot water, thrown in the air, will explode into a cloud of ice particles.

The North Pole is located in the middle of the Arctic Ocean and is usually covered by ice.

The South Pole is at the bottom of our planet on the continent of Antarctica. This region is even colder than the Arctic, sometimes plunging to −125°F (−87.2°C). In winter, parts of the oceans surrounding Antarctica freeze over, doubling its size. Antarctica is the coldest, driest, windiest place on Earth. It is so isolated that no human had even seen this continent until two hundred years ago.

✔ **STOP AND THINK**

Main Ideas and Details Which details on this page help support the main idea that Antarctica is an extremely cold place?

The ice covering Antarctica contains about 70 percent of the world's freshwater.

Places this cold, this extreme, are hard to imagine. In fall the sun sets and doesn't rise again for the entire winter. Months later, it shines twenty-four hours a day— all summer long.

Even though they are covered by ice, these regions are deserts—dry like the Sahara. Very little snow falls in either place. But when it does, it rarely melts. Over time, the snow becomes ice—in some places, almost three miles (5 km) thick.

Icebergs can be as small as a piano or larger than a small country.

This ice is slowly moving, inching from the middle of the Arctic and Antarctica to their coasts. By the time pieces break off into the ocean and become icebergs, the ice is 100,000 years old.

People fly thousands of miles to reach the Poles. And when the winds kick up and blow the snow around, it's hard to know where the sky ends and the land begins. Pilots say that it's like flying inside a Ping-Pong ball.

Many of the instruments normally used to guide planes won't work there. In fact, navigators flying to the Poles are the only ones left in the U.S. Air Force who still help map their route with the stars. This is some of the hardest flying there is.

STOP AND THINK

Author's Craft What do the pilots mean when they say that flying in the Poles is like flying inside a Ping-Pong ball?

Planes do not land in these wintry worlds by rolling down concrete runways. They use skis instead. And they slide like giant sleds until they stop. Gliding along, the skis get so hot that they melt the snow they're resting on. Pilots must pull them up when the planes stop. Otherwise, the wet snow would refreeze on the skis and the planes would be stuck to the ground.

When pilots land at the South Pole, they keep their engines running. It's so cold that they might not start up again.

It sounds like an adventure story, doesn't it? It *is* an adventure story—one with science. Scientists are today's explorers, braving the wilderness to learn more about our world.

The snow near the North Pole, for example, hasn't melted since the last ice age. Over 100,000 years of it has been pressed into an ice sheet almost 2 miles (3.2 km) thick. But each layer looks separate, like the rings of a tree.

Some scientists use this snow to measure air pollution. Others are drilling through this ice to pull out history. Each sample they bring up tells a story about the time when it was formed. Scientists have found volcanic ash from Italy's Mount Vesuvius, for instance, and pollution from ancient Roman times.

Scientists began this experiment to learn more about how ice ages begin and end. Before, they thought our climate needed thousands of years to change. Now they know it can happen much, much faster.

Summit Snow 01
1671

At the South Pole some scientists search for meteorites, rocks from outer space. Meteorites are no more likely to fall there than anywhere else on Earth. But, as one scientist explains, if you want to find something dark, it's easier to look on a big white sheet. His team has given thousands of meteorites to our space agency, the National Aeronautics and Space Administration (NASA), for study.

The Antarctic sky is a perfect window to the stars, the best on this planet. It is very clear because it's so cold and dry—and has a night that is six months long. Some scientists use telescopes to study the age of the universe. Others fly balloons to measure rays coming in from outer space.

At the Poles people wear many layers of clothing to keep warmth in and wind out. They wear big boots and overalls called fat-boy pants. Their mittens have furry backs to wipe their noses and warm their ears.

They also wear goggles. Without them, their eyes would get sunburned and temporarily blinded by the strong light bouncing off the snow.

No wearing rings, earrings, or sunglasses with metal frames in the extreme cold. Metal gets so cold that it will freeze any skin that it touches.

The body is like a furnace that needs fuel to keep running. It works so hard to stay warm at the poles that people end up eating at least twice as much food as usual.

People who work at the Poles must learn how to survive being stuck outdoors. On an <mark>unexpected</mark> "camping trip," they first build a quick <mark>shelter</mark> to get out of the wind. Then they build a better one and pack in close to one another, using body heat to stay warm.

Building shelters—doing any work—is much harder in extreme cold. Mittens are very bulky, but it's unsafe to go bare-handed for long. Getting too cold is dangerous, but so is getting <mark>overheated</mark>. Sweat can freeze into a <mark>layer</mark> of ice next to your body.

In summer many people live at the science stations in the Arctic and Antarctica. They have a gym and videos and spend their spare time skiing on the icy runways. But mostly they work hard, getting as much done as possible while the weather is warm enough for planes to fly in and out.

A few of them stay all winter long. Scientists say that summer's ==constant== daylight tricks your body into wanting to keep going without rest. But in winter's endless darkness, you feel tired much of the time. One scientist even studies the people who winter-over at the South Pole. He wants to know what kind of person works well in such a small, isolated group. Someday his findings may help pick the people to live in a ==colony== on Mars.

STOP AND THINK
Infer/Predict From the description of the Arctic or Antarctica, what can you infer about living on Mars?

Unlike most refrigerators, the one containing fruit and vegetables at the South Pole is heated.

In spring in Antarctica, the temperature finally climbs up to +10°F (−10°C) and it's warm enough for planes to fly in again. The scientists are eager to get on board and return to the colors and smells of the "green world." Once they buckle up, there is one last frosty problem to solve. The airplane must go 100 miles (160 km) per hour to take off, no easy task when sliding over ice. Sometimes pilots must travel 2 miles (3 km) to reach that speed. And sometimes they need extra help. Then they turn to the eight rockets attached to their plane.

A flick of the switch, a burst of flames and speed,
and they are on their way home.

Your Turn

Cold Careers

Write About Your Choice

In *Life on the Ice*, scientists do many different jobs. Which of the jobs do you think is most interesting? Why? Explain your choice.

SOCIAL STUDIES

TV Time

Write a Script Work in a group. Imagine that you are making a TV program about the North or South Pole. Plan three scenes you would show in the program. Sketch each scene. Include some facts to go with each scene. SMALL GROUP

Think Like a Writer

Turn and Talk

Page through *Life on the Ice* with a partner. Discuss the main idea on each page. How do you know what the main ideas are? Are they in the same place every time?

MAIN IDEAS AND DETAILS

Traditional Tales

The Raven: an Inuit Myth

✔ TARGET VOCABULARY

shelter	region
colony	unexpected
constant	gliding
wilderness	overheated
climate	layer

GENRE

A **myth,** like this Readers' Theater, is a story that tells what a group of people believes about the world.

TEXT FOCUS

The **plot** in a myth may explain why or how something in nature came to be. After you read, tell in your own words what this myth explains. Give story details that describe how this natural thing came to be.

Readers' Theater

The Raven:
An Inuit Myth

retold by Peter Case

Cast of Characters

Narrator	**Person**
Old Man	**Raven**

Narrator: Long ago, the People lived in darkness. There was no sun to help things grow. The People called to Raven for help.

Person: Oh, Raven, help us. Our lives are a constant struggle.

Raven: I have heard of an Old Man who has two glowing globes of light. I will try to get these globes.

Narrator: Raven went gliding over the dark wilderness. He came to the shelter where the Old Man lived with his daughter. There, Raven turned himself into a human child.

Old Man: I have a grandson! How wonderful!

Narrator: Raven spoke in the voice of a small child.

Raven: May I please play with the globes of light?

Old Man: Here, grandson, you can play with them.

Narrator: Raven thought of a trick to steal the globes. He pretended he was overheated inside the warm shelter.

Raven: It's so hot inside. I want to take the globes outside.

Old Man: Yes, grandson. You can play outside with the globes.

Narrator: Once Raven was outside, he put on his layer of feathers and flew off with the globes.

Narrator: When he got back to the colony of People, Raven threw the globes up into the sky. One became the sun and the other became the moon. The People were overjoyed.

Person: Now the climate will be good for growing food in this region of the world. Thank you, Raven, for the gift of the sun and for the unexpected gift of the moon.

Making Connections

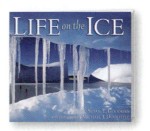

Text to Self

Write a Story Imagine that you are a scientist in Antarctica. Write a short story that tells about your adventures there. Be sure that the story includes details about characters and setting, and an exciting ending that solves a problem in the story.

Text to Text

Discuss Texts Why is the sun so important to the scientists at the Poles and the people in *The Raven*? Talk about this issue in a small group. Listen carefully to one another. Ask each other questions.

Text to World

Connect to Art The art in *The Raven* makes the action in the story more interesting. Look at how the style fits the story. Choose a part of *Life on the Ice* that you like. Make an illustration to go with that passage. Use a style that makes sense for the text.

Grammar

Contractions You know that a **contraction** is a word made by putting two words together. An apostrophe replaces the letter or letters that are left out.

Two Words	Contraction
is not	isn't
have not	haven't
will not	won't
cannot	can't
I am	I'm
she is	she's
they are	they're
you will	you'll
he has	he's
should have	should've

 **Write the contraction for each of the words below.**

❶ are not   ❹ he will

❷ did not   ❺ they have

❸ we are   ❻ it is

Conventions When you write, use contractions. This will make your writing more interesting to read.

Without a Contraction	With the Contraction *n't*
Even in the coldest months, penguins **do not** leave Antarctica.	Even in the coldest months, penguins **don't** leave Antarctica.

Without a Contraction	With Pronoun and Verb Contraction
I am wondering if scientists get gloomy during Antarctica's dark winter.	**I'm** wondering if scientists get gloomy during Antarctica's dark winter.

Connect Grammar to Writing

As you edit your persuasive essay, make sure you have written contractions correctly.

Write to Persuade

✅ **Organization** A **persuasive essay** explains reasons in detail. To help readers follow along, each reason has its own paragraph, starting with transition words, such as "Another reason..."

Daniel drafted his essay about joining a club. Later, he separated his reasons into paragraphs and added transition words.

Writing Process Checklist

Prewrite

Draft

▶ **Revise**

- ✅ Did I begin by telling my goal?
- ✅ Did I give strong reasons?
- ✅ Did I support my reasons with details and examples?
- ✅ Do my new paragraphs use transition words?
- ✅ Did I sum up my reasons in a concluding statement?

Edit

Publish and Share

Revised Draft

Do you love penguins? If your answer is yes, join the Penguin Club! ⁋The main reason to join is that It's fun and interesting. We visit the penguin exhibit at the Science Museum, see live penguins at the Aquarium, and do projects. You'll learn lots of cool penguin facts. For example, did you know that penguins go sledding on their stomachs?

The Penguin Club Is Cool!

by Daniel Singh

Do you love penguins? If your answer is yes, join the Penguin Club!

The main reason to join is that it's fun and interesting. We visit the penguin exhibit at the Science Museum, see live penguins at the Aquarium, and do projects. You'll learn lots of cool penguin facts. For example, did you know that penguins go sledding on their stomachs?

Another great reason to join the club is that penguins need your help. In some parts of the world, penguins have fewer safe, healthy places to live because of changes caused by people.

> I began a new paragraph for each reason. I was also careful to write contractions correctly.

Reading as a Writer

Why did Daniel divide his essay into paragraphs? In your paper, where should you divide your writing into paragraphs?

Clean, Green, and Beautiful

Like Judy Moody in *A Mr. Rubbish Mood*, people everywhere want to do all they can for our planet. Read one boy's ideas in the blog below. Then think about what you can do for your school.

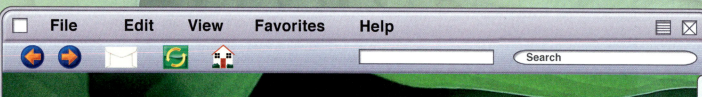

| File | Edit | View | Favorites | Help |

Search

Green Blog

We're on a Roll!

Thanks to teams of "litter scene investigators," our school is litter-free. This is no time to stop. We're on a roll! We can do more!

✿ Start recycling. Recycling paper is a no-brainer in a school! Other things to recycle include cans and plastic bottles.

✿ Start planting trees. Do you know that trees help to reduce air pollution? They can also cut the cost of air conditioning. Trees cost money, so let's start planning fundraisers right away!

Learn more about the Keep Arkansas Beautiful campaign http://www.keeparkansasbeautiful.com/

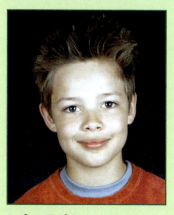

Jaden Baker

Washington Elementary School

Grade 3

posted April 2

Post a comment
View all comments

Log In

Collaborate

Think about what you read in Jaden's blog on page 166. Then talk with a partner about these questions.

- ✔ Is our school litter-free? Why or why not?
- ✔ What does our school recycle? How could we do more?
- ✔ What part of our neighborhood needs more trees?
- ✔ What are some other ways to help our school environment?

Solve a Problem

Choose one way to help your school environment. Work with a partner to plan how to share your idea with others in your school. Let them know how they can help.

How to Help Our Environment
Clean up litter
~~Recycle~~
~~Plant trees~~

How will we let others know?
morning announcements
school assembly

Why should people help?
Litter is dirty and ugly.
Litter can hurt animals.

What do we need?
trash bags
litter sticks or gloves

Who can help?

Unit **4** Wrap-Up

The Big 💡 Idea

Amazing Nature Make a poster about something in nature that you think is amazing. It can be an amazing animal, plant, landform, or body of water. Write two sentences that tell why this part of nature is so interesting to you.

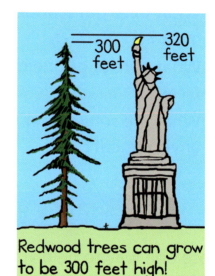

Redwood trees can grow to be 300 feet high!

Listening and Speaking

Tall Tales Some stories are too amazing to be true! Work with a partner to come up with a tall tale based on something you did during a school vacation. Take turns telling each part of the story to the class.

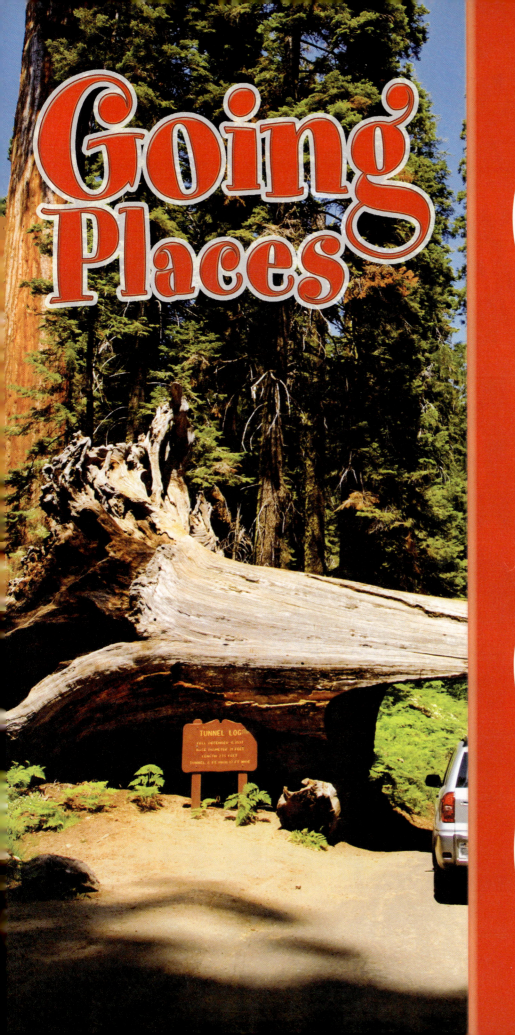

Going Places

Unit 5

Big Idea

There are many
reasons to take
a journey.

Paired Selections

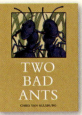

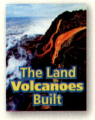
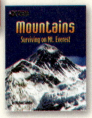

TWO BAD ANTS
CHRIS VAN ALLSBURG

Poems About Bugs

✓ TARGET VOCABULARY

scout

narrow

surrounded

underground

puzzling

glassy

violently

liquid

soggy

unaware

Vocabulary
Reader

Context
Cards

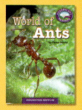
World of Ants

Vocabulary in Context

1 scout

This <mark>scout</mark> explores ahead of the others to lead the way.

2 narrow

In <mark>narrow</mark> spaces, explorers must walk in a single line to get through.

3 surrounded

This island is <mark>surrounded</mark> by water. You need a boat to get there.

4 underground

Exploring these <mark>underground</mark> caves means going down into the earth.

- Study each Context Card.
- Make up a new context sentence that uses two Vocabulary words.

5 **puzzling**

This street sign is so puzzling, or confusing, that drivers may get lost.

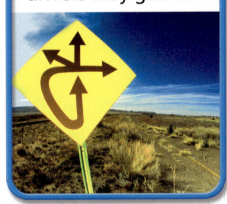

6 **glassy**

The surface of this lake is smooth and glassy. It reflects the boat like a mirror.

7 **violently**

If the wind blows too violently, the tree could blow down.

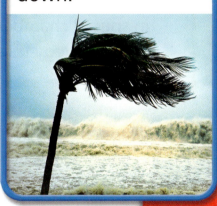

8 **liquid**

It's smart to bring lots of liquid, such as water, on a long hike.

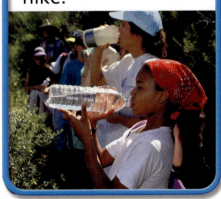

9 **soggy**

Food and clothing get wet and soggy when campers are caught in the rain.

10 **unaware**

The bear looks unaware of the people. It acts as if no one is there.

Background

Ant Life Watching a line of ants disappear underground can be puzzling. Where do they go?

Ants live in narrow, linked tunnels called colonies. Each ant has a job to do. The queen lays eggs. She is surrounded by soldier ants. They violently defend their busy home from attack. Worker ants dig tunnels. Outside the tunnel, scout ants search for food. Ants store food in special chambers, or rooms. This keeps the food from getting soggy if rain or another liquid floods their home.

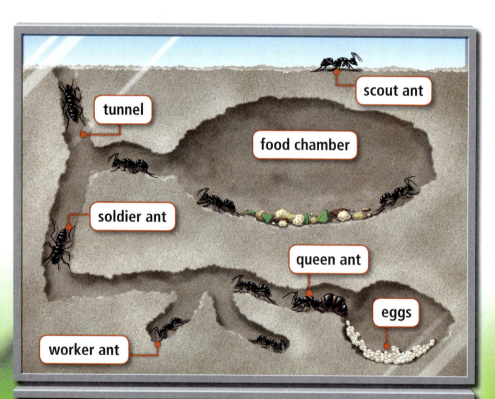

tunnel

scout ant

food chamber

soldier ant

queen ant

eggs

worker ant

Ant Colony

Some ants live between glassy walls in an ant farm. They seem unaware of humans watching their community in action. How many kinds of ants are shown here?

Comprehension

Pay attention to the setting and the characters in *Two Bad Ants*. Then use story details to identify the plot. What problem do the characters face, and how do they find a solution? Show the story structure in *Two Bad Ants* in a story map like this one.

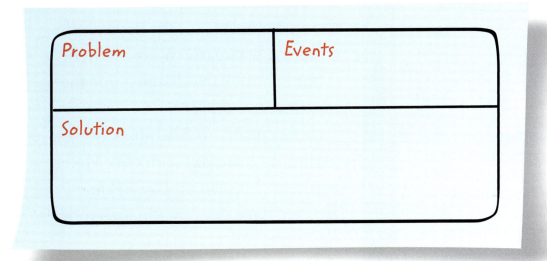

Problem	Events
Solution	

✔ **TARGET STRATEGY** **Monitor/Clarify**

In *Two Bad Ants*, the author tells what story characters *think* is happening, not what is *really* happening. Readers must figure out story events on their own. When story events are confusing, try reading the text again or read ahead to figure out what is really happening to the ants.

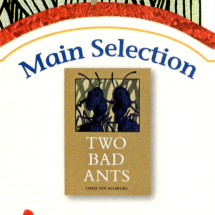

TWO BAD ANTS
CHRIS VAN ALLSBURG

scout	glassy
narrow	violently
surrounded	liquid
underground	soggy
puzzling	unaware

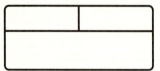
✔ TARGET SKILL

Story Structure Name the setting, character, and plot in a story. Say whether the story is told in the first or third person.

✔ TARGET STRATEGY

Monitor/Clarify As you read, find a way to clear up what doesn't make sense.

GENRE

A **fantasy** is a story that could not happen in real life.

MEET THE AUTHOR AND ILLUSTRATOR

Chris Van Allsburg

One morning Chris Van Allsburg came downstairs in his Rhode Island home to find two ants on the kitchen countertop. He began to imagine the strange journey the little insects might have made from his backyard to his kitchen. That is how Van Allsburg got the idea for *Two Bad Ants*.

Several of Van Allsburg's books, including his two Caldecott Medal winners, *Jumanji* and *The Polar Express*, have been made into movies.

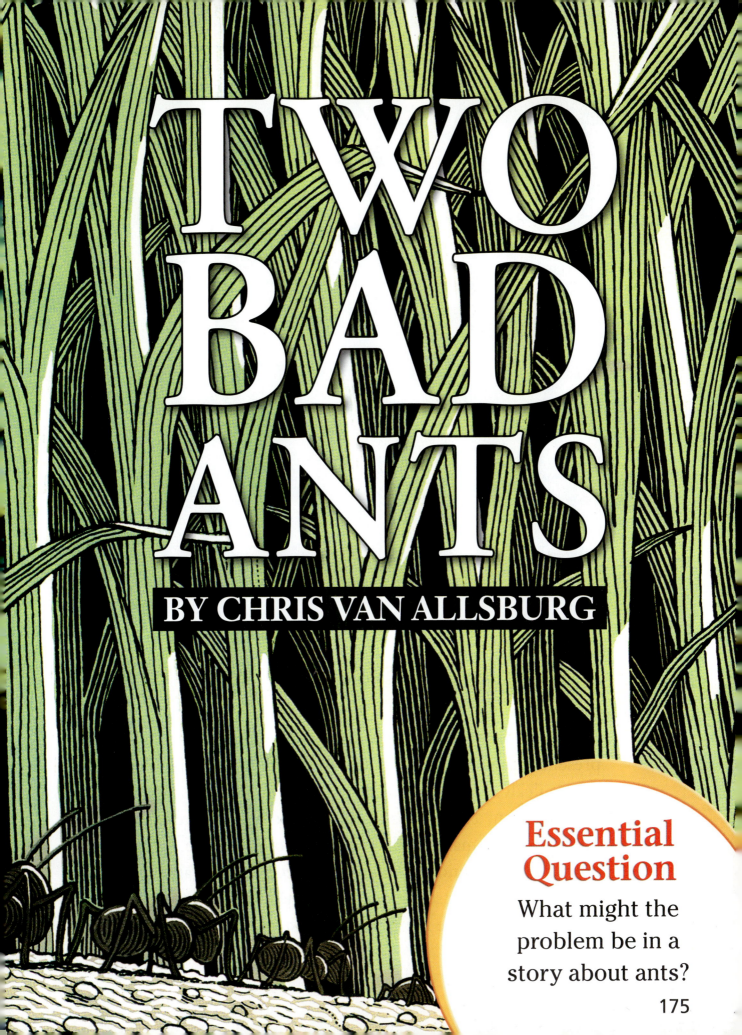

TWO BAD ANTS

BY CHRIS VAN ALLSBURG

Essential Question

What might the problem be in a story about ants?

175

The news traveled swiftly through the tunnels of the ant world. A <mark>scout</mark> had returned with a remarkable discovery—a beautiful sparkling crystal. When the scout presented the crystal to the ant queen she took a small bite, then quickly ate the entire thing.

She deemed it the most delicious food she had ever tasted. Nothing could make her happier than to have more, much more. The ants understood. They were eager to gather more crystals because the queen was the mother of them all. Her happiness made the whole ant nest a happy place.

It was late in the day when they departed. Long shadows stretched over the entrance to the ant kingdom. One by one the insects climbed out, following the scout, who had made it clear—there were many crystals where the first had been found, but the journey was long and dangerous.

They marched into the woods that surrounded their underground home. Dusk turned to twilight, twilight to night. The path they followed twisted and turned, every bend leading them deeper into the dark forest.

More than once the line of ants stopped and anxiously listened for the sounds of hungry spiders. But all they heard was the call of crickets echoing through the woods like distant thunder.

Dew formed on the leaves above. Without warning, huge cold drops fell on the marching ants. A firefly passed overhead that, for an instant, lit up the woods with a blinding flash of blue-green light.

At the edge of the forest stood a mountain. The ants looked up and could not see its peak. It seemed to reach right to the heavens. But they did not stop. Up the side they climbed, higher and higher.

The wind whistled through the cracks of the mountain's face. The ants could feel its force bending their delicate antennae. Their legs grew weak as they struggled upward. At last they reached a ledge and crawled through a **narrow** tunnel.

STOP AND THINK

Monitor/Clarify The story says the ants are in the woods, then on a mountain. How do you know the ants aren't really there?

When the ants came out of the tunnel they found themselves in a strange world. Smells they had known all their lives, smells of dirt and grass and rotting plants, had vanished. There was no more wind and, most puzzling of all, it seemed that the sky was gone.

They crossed smooth shiny surfaces, then followed the scout up a glassy, curved wall. They had reached their goal. From the top of the wall they looked below to a sea of crystals. One by one the ants climbed down into the sparkling treasure.

Quickly they each chose a crystal, then turned to start the journey home. There was something about this unnatural place that made the ants nervous. In fact they left in such a hurry that none of them noticed the two small ants who stayed behind.

"Why go back?" one asked the other. "This place may not feel like home, but look at all these crystals." "You're right," said the other, "we can stay here and eat this tasty treasure every day, forever." So the two ants ate crystal after crystal until they were too full to move, and fell asleep.

Daylight came. The sleeping ants were <mark>unaware</mark> of changes taking place in their new found home. A giant silver scoop hovered above them, then plunged deep into the crystals. It shoveled up both ants and crystals and carried them high into the air.

The ants were wide awake when the scoop turned, dropping them from a frightening height. They tumbled through space in a shower of crystals and fell into a boiling brown lake.

Then the giant scoop stirred <mark>violently</mark> back and forth.
Crushing waves fell over the ants. They paddled hard
to keep their tiny heads above water. But the scoop kept
spinning the hot brown <mark>liquid</mark>.

Around and around it went, creating a whirlpool that
sucked the ants deeper and deeper. They both held their
breath and finally bobbed to the surface, gasping for air and
spitting mouthfuls of the terrible, bitter water.

Then the lake tilted and began to empty into a cave. The ants could hear the rushing water and felt themselves pulled toward the pitch black hole. Suddenly the cave disappeared and the lake became calm. The ants swam to the shore and found that the lake had steep sides.

They hurried down the walls that held back the lake. The frightened insects looked for a place to hide, worried that the giant scoop might shovel them up again. Close by they found a huge round disk with holes that could neatly hide them.

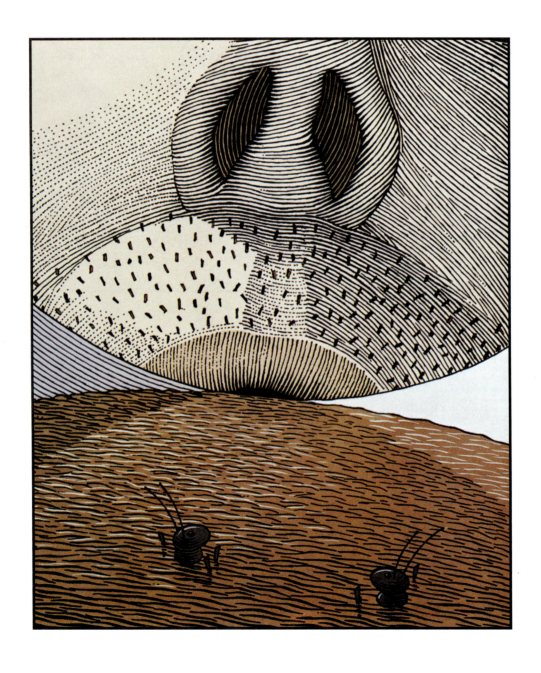

But as soon as they climbed inside, their hiding place was lifted, tilted, and lowered into a dark space. When the ants climbed out of the holes they were surrounded by a strange red glow. It seemed to them that every second the temperature was rising.

It soon became so unbearably hot that they thought they would soon be cooked. But suddenly the disk they were standing on rocketed upward and the two hot ants went flying through the air.

STOP AND THINK

Author's Craft The author tells the story from the ants' point of view. How would the story be different if it were told from a person's point of view?

They landed near what seemed to be a fountain—a waterfall pouring from a silver tube. Both ants had a powerful thirst and longed to dip their feverish heads into the fresh water. They quickly climbed along the tube.

As they got closer to the rushing water the ants felt a cool spray. They tightly gripped the shiny surface of the fountain and slowly leaned their heads into the falling stream. But the force of the water was much too strong.

The tiny insects were pulled off the fountain and plunged down into a wet, dark chamber. They landed on half-eaten fruit and other soggy things. Suddenly the air was filled with loud, frightening sounds. The chamber began to spin.

The ants were caught in a whirling storm of shredded food and stinging rain. Then, just as quickly as it had started, the noise and spinning stopped. Bruised and dizzy, the ants climbed out of the chamber.

In daylight once again, they raced through puddles and up a smooth metal wall. In the distance they saw something comforting—two long, narrow holes that reminded them of the warmth and safety of their old underground home. They climbed up into the dark openings.

But there was no safety inside these holes. A strange force passed through the wet ants. They were stunned senseless and blown out of the holes. When they landed the tiny insects were too exhausted to go on. They crawled into a dark corner and fell fast asleep.

Night had returned when the battered ants awoke
to a familiar sound—the footsteps of their fellow insects
returning for more crystals. The two ants slipped quietly to
the end of the line. They climbed the glassy wall and once
again stood amid the treasure. But this time they each chose
a single crystal and followed their friends home.

Standing at the edge of their ant hole, the two ants listened to the joyful sounds that came from below. They knew how grateful their mother queen would be when they gave her their crystals. At that moment, the two ants felt happier than they'd ever felt before. This was their home, this was their family. This was where they were meant to be.

✔ STOP AND THINK

Story Structure How might the ending be different if the ants' adventures had been more fun and less scary?

Your Turn

An Ant's Eye View

Write a Paragraph In *Two Bad Ants*, the ants think that a house is a mountain. Write sentences about other items the ants are wrong about. Why do you think the author chose to write the story from the ants' point of view?

AUTHOR'S CRAFT

The ants think that a house is a mountain.

Return of the Ants!

Draw a Cartoon What will the two bad ants do next? With a partner, imagine their next adventure. Then plan and sketch a cartoon of what happens to them. Include speech balloons.

PARTNERS

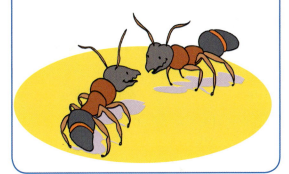

Problems, Problems

Turn and Talk

With a partner, find the place in the story where the two ants' problems begin. Discuss how their problems develop, grow, and are solved. Would you have ended the story the same way? STORY STRUCTURE

Poetry

Poems About
Bugs

✓ **TARGET VOCABULARY**

scout	glassy
narrow	violently
surrounded	liquid
underground	soggy
puzzling	unaware

GENRE

Poetry uses the sound and rhythm of words to show images and express feelings. Discuss how these poets use sound and rhythm in their poems to help you picture what is being described.

TEXT FOCUS

Poets may use **alliteration**, which is repeating the beginning sounds of words, to make the poems more fun to read.

Poems About Bugs

The poems you will read next are about bugs. The first poem is a limerick by Edward Lear. A limerick is a short, funny poem with five lines. The first, second, and fifth lines rhyme. So do the third and fourth lines.

A Limerick

There was an Old Man in a tree,
Who was horribly bored by a Bee;
When they said, 'Does it buzz?'
He replied, 'Yes, it does!'
'It's a regular brute of a Bee!'

by Edward Lear

Honeybees live in hives. They enter the hive through **narrow** openings. Honeybees make a thick, sweet **liquid** called honey.

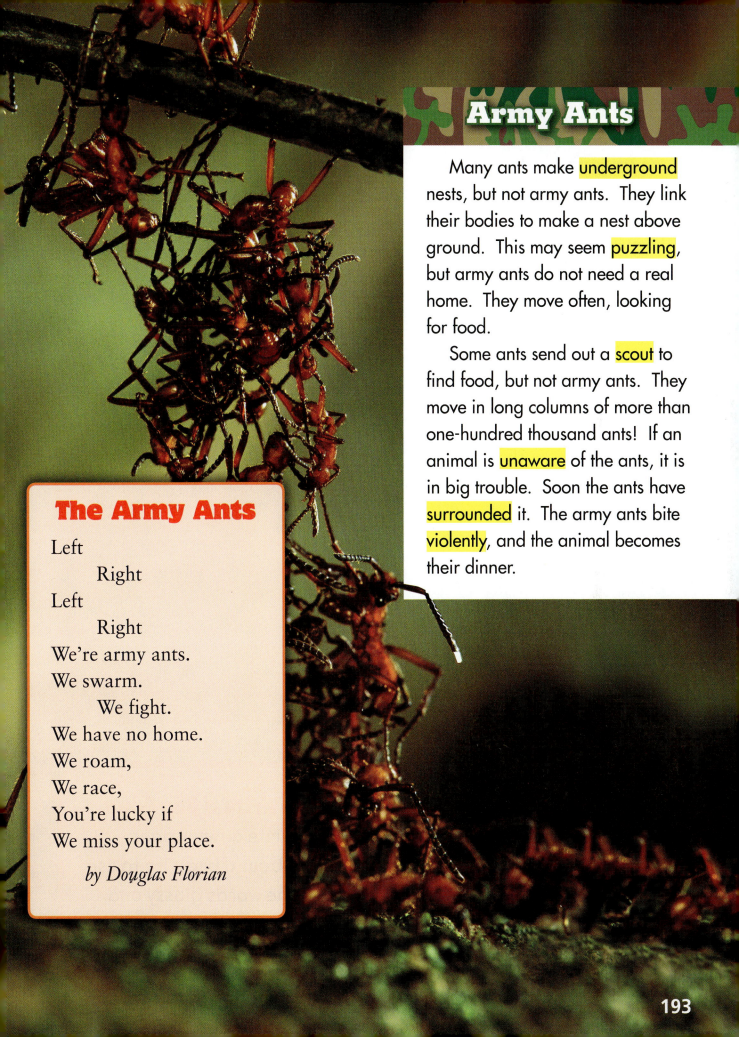

Army Ants

Many ants make underground nests, but not army ants. They link their bodies to make a nest above ground. This may seem puzzling, but army ants do not need a real home. They move often, looking for food.

Some ants send out a scout to find food, but not army ants. They move in long columns of more than one-hundred thousand ants! If an animal is unaware of the ants, it is in big trouble. Soon the ants have surrounded it. The army ants bite violently, and the animal becomes their dinner.

The Army Ants

Left
     Right
Left
     Right
We're army ants.
We swarm.
     We fight.
We have no home.
We roam,
We race,
You're lucky if
We miss your place.

by Douglas Florian

Upside Down

It's funny how beetles
and creatures like that
can walk upside down
as well as walk flat.

They crawl on a ceiling
and climb on a wall
without any practice
or trouble at all,

While *I* have been trying
for a year (maybe more)
and still I can't stand
with my head on the floor.

by Aileen Fisher

Write a Bug Poem

Write a funny poem
about a bug. Try to use
the words **glassy** and
soggy in your poem.

194

Making Connections

 Text to Self

Write a Story What adventures would the ants in *Two Bad Ants* have in your kitchen? Write a story in the style of *Two Bad Ants* that tells what would happen. Include details about the setting. Build the story to an exciting finish.

 Text to Text

Compare Texts Read the Aesop's tale *The Ant and the Dove*, either in a library book or on the Internet. In a small group, discuss how the lessons the characters learn in this tale and in *Two Bad Ants* are alike and different.

 Text to World

All About Ants On the Internet or in reference books, do research about ants. Find out where they live, what they eat, how they build their homes, and other details about their lives. Prepare a report for your class on your findings.

Grammar

Possessive Nouns and Possessive Pronouns A **possessive noun** shows that a person or an animal owns or has something. Add an apostrophe and -s ('s) to a singular noun to make it a possessive noun. Add an apostrophe to a plural noun that ends in s (s') to make it a possessive noun.

Academic Language

possessive noun

possessive pronoun

Noun	Possessive Noun
mother	mother's face
insect	insect's wings

A pronoun that shows ownership is a **possessive pronoun**.

my   your   her   his   its   our   their

 **Write the possessive form of each underlined noun.**

1 queen wish

3 many chefs hats

2 several parents toasters

4 ant antenna

Write each sentence and underline the possessive pronoun.

5 Beth left her book on the table.

6 David and Sebastian are riding their new bikes.

Ideas When you write, you can make a sentence clearer by adding a possessive noun or possessive pronoun that tells more about the subject. Put the possessive noun or pronoun and any words that go with it right after the subject. Use a comma before and after the words you add.

Less Clear Sentence	Clearer Sentence
Willa watched the ants in her ant farm.	Willa, John's sister, watched the ants in her ant farm.

Less Clear Sentence:	The ant farm won first prize in the science fair.
Clearer Sentence:	The ant farm, which is mine, won first prize in the science fair.

Connect Grammar to Writing

As you revise your story paragraph, check to see if you can make your sentences clearer. Add possessive nouns and possessive pronouns to tell more about your subjects.

Write to Express

☑️ **Ideas** As you read *Two Bad Ants*, were you anxious to find out what would happen next? That feeling is called suspense. Writers create suspense in their stories by giving hints about what *might* happen. See if you can add some suspense to your own **story** paragraphs.

Holly wrote a scene about a brave mouse. Later, she added some details that created more suspense.

Writing Traits Checklist

☑️ **Ideas**
Did I add suspense to my story?

☑️ **Organization**
Do the characters face problems they have to solve?

☑️ **Word Choice**
Did I use vivid words?

☑️ **Voice**
Did I include dialogue?

☑️ **Sentence Fluency**
Did I use both simple and compound sentences?

☑️ **Conventions**
Did I edit for correct grammar?

Revised Draft

"Oh what should I do?" squeaked Emily Mouse. It had poured, and the street was a river. Emily was afraid of water, **and couldn't swim** but she had to get across. Clara was on the other side **. Emily's baby, caught in a trap**. Soon Emily saw a **rusty old** tuna can floating toward her. She found a flat little stick, jumped into the can, and began paddling. Emily was too busy to feel her tail and feet getting soaked.

The Bravest Mouse

by Holly Becker

"Oh what should I do?" squeaked Emily Mouse. It had poured, and the street was a river. Emily was afraid of water and couldn't swim, but she had to get across. Clara, Emily's baby, was on the other side caught in a trap. Soon Emily saw a rusty old tuna can floating toward her. She found a flat little stick, jumped into the can, and began paddling. Emily was too busy to feel her tail and feet getting soaked. Suddenly, the leaky can sank. Emily's paddle floated away. She began kicking and paddling with her feet. "Hey, I'm swimming!" she thought. "Hang on, Clara. Here I come!"

I added details that helped build suspense. I also added nouns to a sentence to tell more about the subject.

Reading as a Writer

Which details add suspense to Holly's story? Where can you add suspense in your own story?

TARGET VOCABULARY

migrate

survival

plenty

frightening

accidents

solid

chilly

landscape

thunderous

dramatic

Vocabulary Reader   Context Cards

Vocabulary in Context

1   migrate
These butterflies fly far away when they <mark>migrate</mark>, or move from place to place.

2   survival
This bluebird flies south for the winter for its <mark>survival</mark>, or to stay alive.

3   plenty
Some animals don't migrate in winter if they have saved <mark>plenty</mark> of food.

4   frightening
It is <mark>frightening</mark>, or scary, for penguins when leopard seals come nearby.

- Study each **Context Card**.
- Use two Vocabulary words to tell about an experience you had.

5 accidents

When moose cross busy roads to find food, **accidents** can happen.

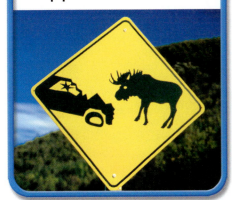

6 solid

It is very hard for animals to find food under snow and **solid** ice.

7 chilly

Polar bears have thick fur to keep them warm in cold, **chilly** weather.

8 landscape

The **landscape** changes in spring. Grass turns green, and flowers bloom.

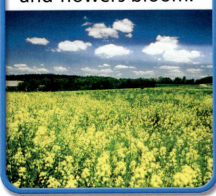

9 thunderous

A herd of caribou makes a very loud, **thunderous** sound as it runs.

10 dramatic

Salmon swimming upstream to lay eggs is a **dramatic**, or exciting, sight.

Background

✓ **TARGET VOCABULARY**   **Migration** Every year, animals migrate. Survival often depends on finding new ways to get enough food, water, or shelter. There may be plenty to eat or drink in one spot during summer but none in the chilly winter. Rivers can freeze into solid ice. As a result, animals must migrate in order to survive.

Sometimes thousands of animals migrate together. This can be a frightening and dramatic sight. They may make a thunderous noise as they cross the landscape. Both animals and people must be careful to avoid accidents!

This map shows the major routes some birds follow when they migrate across North America to warmer southern climates. How many different major routes do you see?

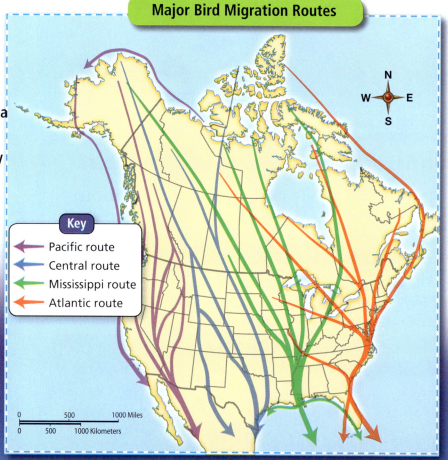

Major Bird Migration Routes

Key
- Pacific route
- Central route
- Mississippi route
- Atlantic route

0   500   1000 Miles
0   500   1000 Kilometers

Comprehension

Compare and Contrast

Find out how a locust's migration compares to that of a gray whale. What is the same, and what is different about these experiences? Use a Venn diagram like this one to compare details about how locusts and whales migrate.

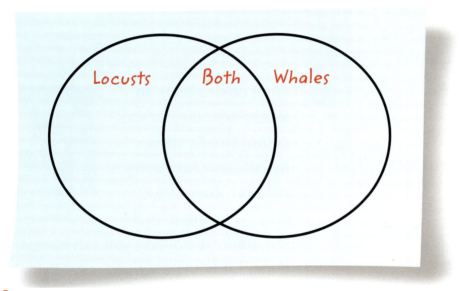

Locusts   Both   Whales

✔ **TARGET STRATEGY** **Visualize**

Use the information in your Venn diagram to help you visualize, or picture, details about whales and locusts. How do they look, sound, and act as they migrate?

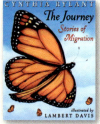

✓ **TARGET VOCABULARY**

migrate	solid
survival	chilly
plenty	landscape
frightening	thunderous
accidents	dramatic

✓ **TARGET SKILL**

Compare and Contrast

Tell how details or ideas are alike and different.

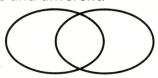

✓ **TARGET STRATEGY**

Visualize As you read, use selection details to picture what is happening.

GENRE

Informational text gives factual information about a topic. Use what you know about genre to set a purpose for reading.

MEET THE AUTHOR

Cynthia Rylant

What advice does an award-winning, famous author like Cynthia Rylant have for young writers? Go out and play. "Playing is still the greatest training you can have, I think, for being a writer," says Rylant. "It helps you love life, it helps you relax, and it helps you cook up interesting stuff in your head." She is the author of *The Blue Hill Meadows* and many other books.

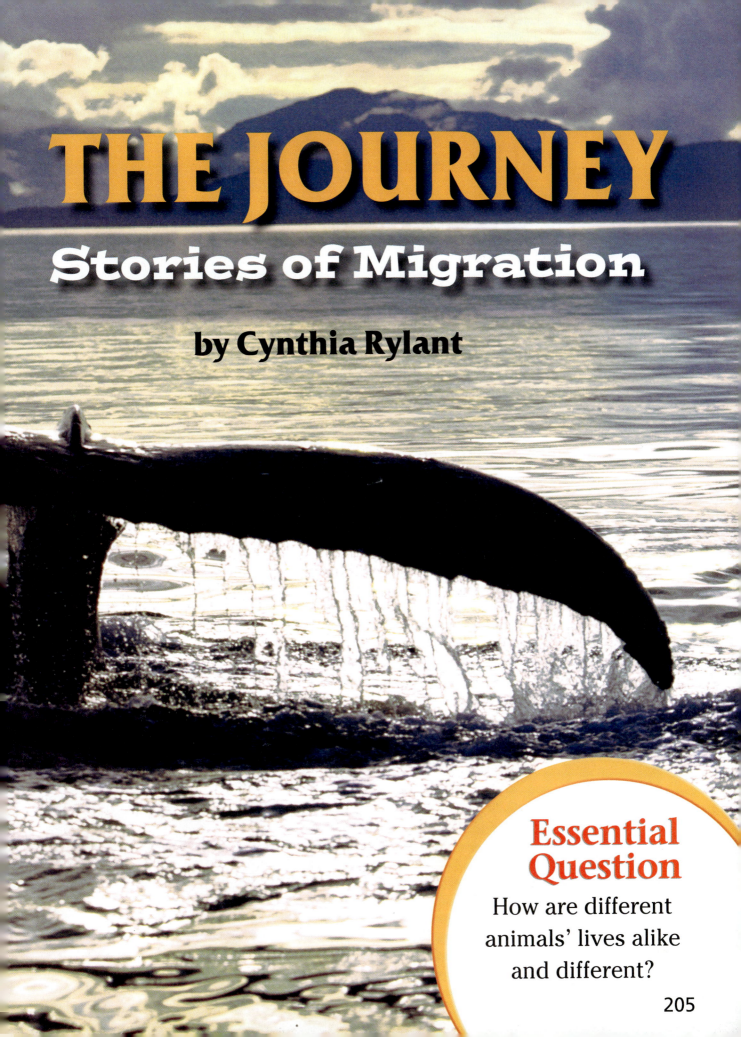

THE JOURNEY
Stories of Migration

by Cynthia Rylant

Introduction

Most creatures live out their lives in the places where they are born. The tiny mouse runs in the fields where his mother ran. The gray squirrel lives in the same tall trees all her life. The cow stays on the farm.

But there are some creatures who do not stay where they are born, who cannot stay. These are the creatures who <mark>migrate</mark>. Their lives will be spent moving from one place to another. Some will migrate to survive. Some will migrate to create new life. All will be remarkable.

Here are the stories of two of these remarkable travelers—so different from each other but so alike in one profound way: Each must *move*.

The Locusts

There are few migrations as <mark>dramatic</mark> and <mark>frightening</mark> as when the desert locusts are moving across Africa. These insects are actually young grasshoppers, and grasshoppers usually do not travel.

But sometimes too many grasshopper eggs are laid in one small area, and when the grasshoppers are born, there isn't enough food. The grasshoppers now have only one choice for <mark>survival</mark>: to migrate in search of vegetation.

207

And so these grasshoppers will begin changing. Their bodies will turn from light green to dark yellow or red. Their antennae will grow short rather than long. And when they rise up to fly together by the *billions*, they will be grasshoppers no more. They will be locusts.

A cloud of desert locusts in the sky is an unbelievable sight. There are so many locusts that they block out the sun. It seems like night. And in the sudden darkness there is a terrible ==thunderous== noise. It is the noise of a billion wings.

STOP AND THINK

Visualize What words and phrases help you visualize how it looks and sounds when the locusts fly away together?

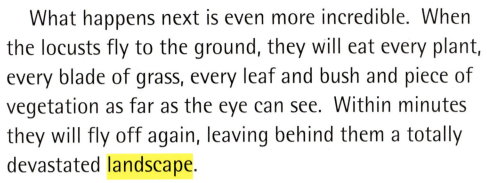

What happens next is even more incredible. When the locusts fly to the ground, they will eat every plant, every blade of grass, every leaf and bush and piece of vegetation as far as the eye can see. Within minutes they will fly off again, leaving behind them a totally devastated landscape.

And though locusts do not willfully hurt people—they want only to eat gardens, trees, bushes, grass—people may die because of the locusts. Because the gardens are empty of food, people may die of starvation.

Desert locusts can also cause <mark>accidents</mark>. Locusts fly very high—as high as two miles up in the sky—and this can make difficult flying for planes that have to move through the locust cloud. The swarms can also interfere with trains. And millions of crushed locusts on a highway will make cars slip and slide.

There are many stories in history about the terrible devastation of locust plagues. It is written that in ancient times, one locust swarm covered 2,000 square miles.

The swarms today are not nearly as large as that. But they can still be quite big, often as much as one hundred square miles. Imagine so many insects in the sky!

locust eggs

As the locusts migrate in search of food, they ride the winds from one area of rainfall to the next. (There is always more food where it rains.) They travel on sunny mornings and stop in late afternoon to roost for the night.

When they reach a rainy area, they mate and die. Then their eggs will hatch and a new swarm of locusts begins moving. This will happen again and again until one day a swarm will return to the same place where the very first locusts began.

And if the eggs laid are not too many, and if there is plenty of food when the new eggs hatch, there will be no locust swarms for a while. Only pale green grasshoppers moving quietly about.

But someday too many eggs may be laid, and the newly hatched grasshoppers will be much too hungry. These grasshoppers will begin to look a little different and act a little different.

Then they will rise up together by the billions—as desert locusts—and they will fly.

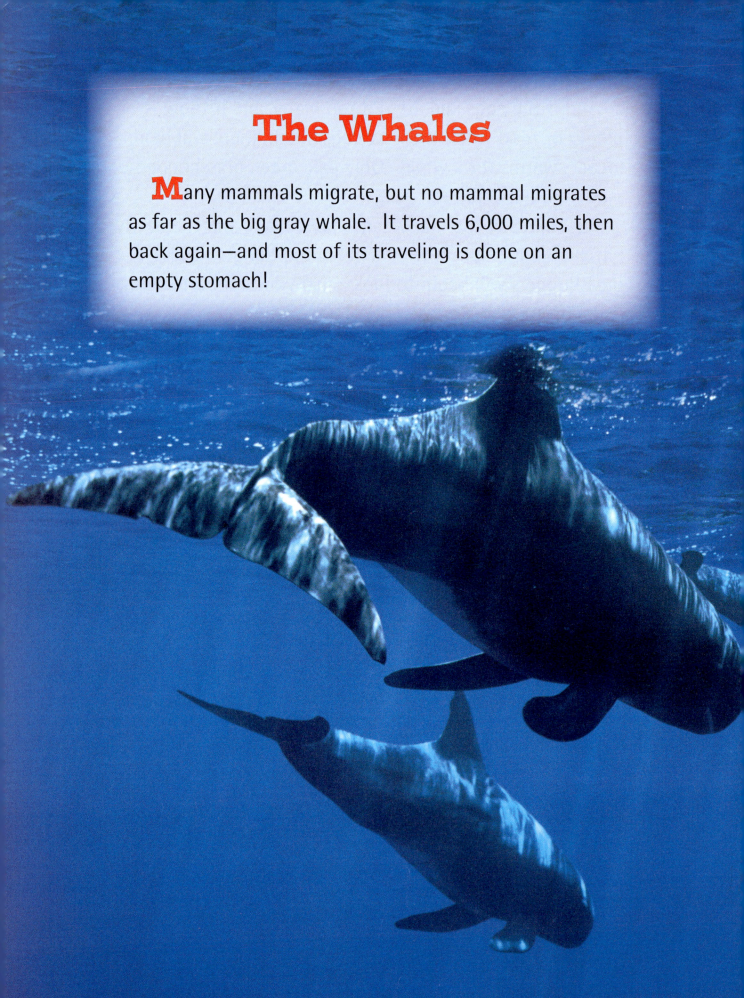

The Whales

Many mammals migrate, but no mammal migrates as far as the big gray whale. It travels 6,000 miles, then back again—and most of its traveling is done on an empty stomach!

Gray whales love the cold waters near the North Pole because the waters are full of the food they love to eat. The whales live on tiny ocean shrimp and worms, and the Arctic waters are full of these in summer. The whales eat and eat and eat, straining the tiny food through strips of baleen in their mouths. (Instead of teeth, the grays have baleen—long strips of a hard material similar to fingernails.)

The gray whales swim and eat mostly alone through the summer. But in the fall, they will begin to look for some traveling companions, because the whales know one thing for certain: that they must migrate. In winter, the Arctic seas are going to be filled with solid ice. And the whales will die if they stay.

The first gray whales to leave the Arctic are the pregnant females. These expectant mothers want to have plenty of time to reach the warm waters of California and Mexico before they give birth. No mother wants to have a baby in icy water!

STOP AND THINK

Author's Craft How does the author make sure readers understand what baleen are and how they work?

215

The other whales will follow, and in small groups they will all travel down the Pacific coast. Once they leave the Arctic, the whales won't find much food again, and it may be as long as *eight months* before they eat.

But the whales have stored a lot of fat in their bodies, called blubber, and this will keep them alive.

As they travel, the whales often swim near shore, and people along the way are thrilled. They wave to the whales from rocky cliffs and travel out in boats to say hello to them.

When finally the gray whales reach the warm tropical waters in January, the pregnant females will give birth. And the other whales will mate.

With new calves among them, all of the whales will enjoy life in the peaceful lagoons for a while. Then in March, they will be ready to head back to the Arctic for the summer. They haven't forgotten how they love to eat there!

This time the males will leave first, and the females and calves will stay behind for another several weeks. The calves will have more time to grow and get stronger for the long journey.

The arrows on the map show the gray whales' 6,000-mile journey from the Arctic, then back again.

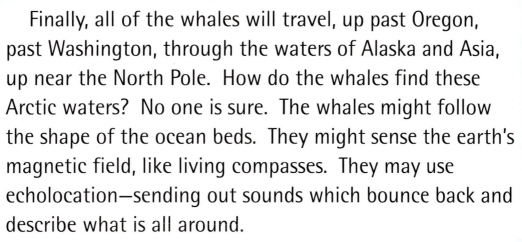

Finally, all of the whales will travel, up past Oregon, past Washington, through the waters of Alaska and Asia, up near the North Pole. How do the whales find these Arctic waters? No one is sure. The whales might follow the shape of the ocean beds. They might sense the earth's magnetic field, like living compasses. They may use echolocation—sending out sounds which bounce back and describe what is all around.

But somehow the whales will travel that long 6,000-mile journey north, and they will find the same chilly waters they left behind. When they arrive in the Arctic, they will separate and enjoy a summer of fine ocean eating.

✔ STOP AND THINK

Compare and Contrast What is the same about the two trips whales make? What is different?

But just before the Arctic winter arrives, before the ice, something will tell the whales to find each other again. To find some company for another long, long swim.

Your Turn

A Close Look

Write a Description
Scientists watch animals closely to learn about them. Think of a time you watched an animal closely. Write a description of where you were and what you saw. What did you learn about the animal? SCIENCE

Before and After

Make a Comparison Work in a small group. Think of a park or green space you know. What would it look like after a swarm of locusts landed there? What would be gone, and what would remain? Draw "before" and "after" pictures. SMALL GROUP

Our Wild World

Turn and Talk With a partner, compare grasshoppers and locusts. How are they alike? How are they different? Next, compare the locusts' migration with the migration of the whales. Which migration do you think is more amazing?

COMPARE AND CONTRAST

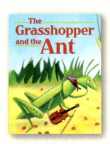

✓ **TARGET VOCABULARY**

migrate	solid
survival	chilly
plenty	landscape
frightening	thunderous
accidents	dramatic

GENRE

A **fable** Is a short story in which a character, usually an animal, learns a lesson.

TEXT FOCUS

A **moral** of a fable is the lesson that a character learns. After reading this fable, use your own words to tell what important lesson the fable teaches.

The Grasshopper and the Ant

an **Aesop's fable** adapted by **Margaretha Rabe**

Grasshopper loved to sing and play his fiddle. He played quiet songs and thunderous tunes. Sometimes Grasshopper played frightening music. Then he would hop around in a dramatic way. That's when he caused accidents.

One time Grasshopper jumped into a pile of grain that Ant had spent all day collecting. The grain scattered across the landscape.

"You should be more careful, Grasshopper," scolded Ant. "I worked hard to gather that grain. Now I have to pile it up again."

"I'm sorry," said Grasshopper. "Why not take a break? It's a beautiful, sunny day. You'll have plenty of days to gather food."

"You may think so, Grasshopper, but winter will soon be here. Then the ground will be frozen solid," said Ant. "Now is the time to gather food and plan for survival. You should take a break from playing and do some work."

Grasshopper said, "I'll migrate to someplace warm if it gets too chilly. That way, I can keep on playing and singing. But for now I'll play any song you like to make your work easier to do."

Weeks later, fat flakes of snow began to drift from the sky. Grasshopper shivered. It was so cold that he could hardly hold his fiddle. Grasshopper looked for food, but the ground had turned into a blanket of white snow.

"What will I do now? I can't find food, and it's too cold for me to go far. Maybe Ant will help me," thought Grasshopper.

Grasshopper trudged through the snow and knocked on Ant's door. "Will you give me food if I sing and play for you?" asked Grasshopper.

Ant said, "Yes I will. I worked hard the rest of the year, so now I have time to relax and have fun."

Moral: There are times to work and times to play.

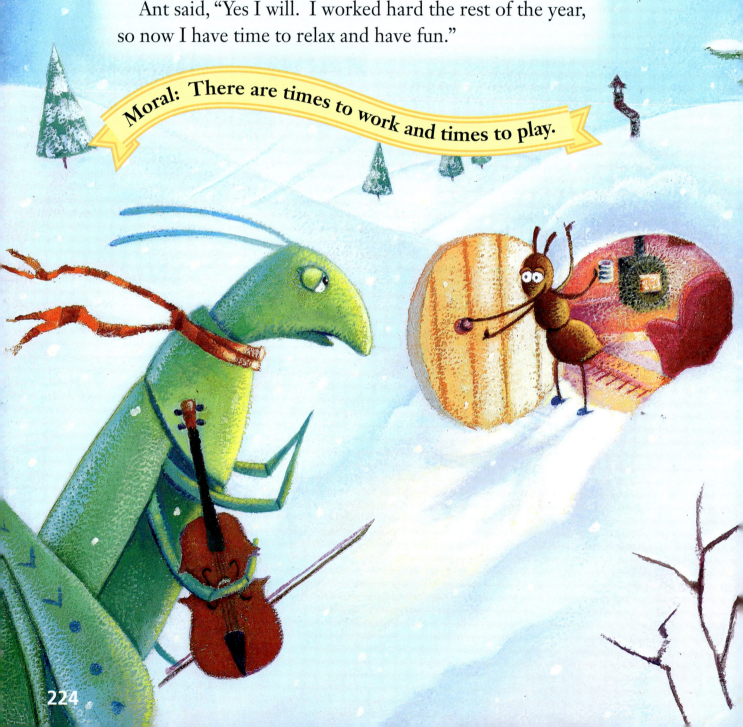

Making Connections

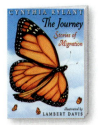 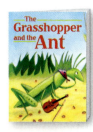

 Text to Self

Grasshopper or Ant? In *Grasshopper and the Ant*, Grasshopper likes to play, and Ant is always working. Are you more like Grasshopper or Ant? Or are you a little bit like both? Write a paragraph explaining your answer and giving examples.

 Text to Text

Have an Interview With a partner, pretend to interview an animal from *The Journey: Stories of Migration* and Ant from *The Grasshopper and the Ant*. Take turns interviewing, asking questions about how each creature prepares for winter. Present your interviews to the class.

 Text to World

Connect to Science You read that locusts and whales migrate. Use the library or Internet to find out about another animal that migrates. Make a poster or other display to show what you learned.

Grammar

Using Proper Nouns There are many kinds of **proper nouns**. Names for days, months, holidays, and titles of people are proper nouns. Always begin a proper noun with a capital letter. Include a comma after the number in dates.

Academic Language

proper noun

Thursday	March
Saturday	December
July 24, 2012	Labor Day
August 10, 1949	Memorial Day
Mrs. Emma J. Lopez	Officer Wilson
Mr. Brian Chang	Governor Peterson

Try This! **Write each sentence correctly. Remember to punctuate the date correctly.**

❶ School will be closed next monday.

❷ It is columbus day.

❸ My teacher, mr. wade, told us about something to do on the day off.

❹ We might see the locust migration on october 8 2011.

❺ doctor ortez will give a talk at the hospital.

Ideas In your writing, you can make a sentence clearer by adding words that tell when. You can also include a proper noun for days, months, or holidays.

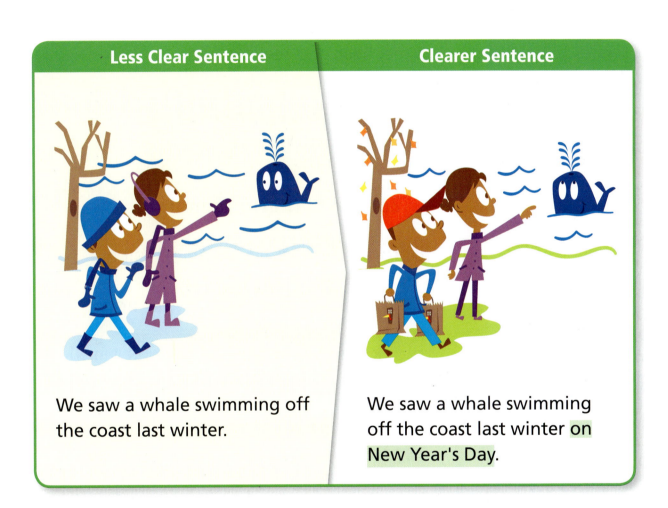

Less Clear Sentence	Clearer Sentence
We saw a whale swimming off the coast last winter.	We saw a whale swimming off the coast last winter on New Year's Day.

✏️ **Grammar in Writing**

As you revise your descriptive paragraph, try to add words that tell when. Be sure to use capital letters, commas, and periods correctly.

Write to Express

In *The Journey: Stories of Migration*, you read that a billion locusts' wings sound like thunder. *Like thunder* is a simile, which is a phrase that uses *like* or *as* to compare two things.

Ethan wrote a **description** of a canary. Later, he added similes to help his readers see, hear, and feel the bird.

Writing Traits Checklist

✔ **Ideas**
Did I use details for at least three of the five senses?

✔ **Organization**
Did I tell my details in a clear order?

✔ **Word Choice**
Did I use similes?

✔ **Voice**
Do my feelings come through?

✔ **Sentence Fluency**
Did I use phrases that tell where and when?

✔ **Conventions**
Did I edit my work for spelling, grammar, and punctuation?

Revised Draft

Zack was a little canary. He belonged to a boy named Mike. Zack was ~~bright yellow.~~ as yellow as the sun. He had black eyes, like tiny glass beads and his beak was small and pointed. Under his beak, his feathers were soft and puffy, like kitten fur but his wings and tail were smooth. He hopped around on ~~skinny~~ legs. as skinny as toothpicks Every morning, Zack had a great voice. He sang loudly and cheerfully.

228

Zack

by Ethan Washington

Zack was a little canary. He belonged to a boy named Mike. Zack was as yellow as the sun. He had black eyes like tiny glass beads, and his beak was small and pointed. Under his beak, his feathers were soft and puffy like kitten fur, but his wings and tail were smooth. He hopped around on legs as skinny as toothpicks. Zack had a great voice. Every morning, he sang loudly and cheerfully. He sounded like a person whistling. Sometimes he liked to perch on Mike's shoulder when he sang. Zack was a happy, friendly bird.

I added similes to help readers picture Zack. I also added a phrase that tells when.

Reading as a Writer

What similes did Ethan use to describe Zack? Where can you add similes in your paper?

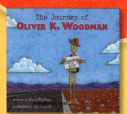

sincere

managed

loaded

loveliest

conversations

inspired

reunion

currently

pleasure

terror

Vocabulary
Reader

Context
Cards

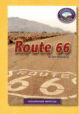

Vocabulary in Context

1 sincere

This President had sincere hopes. He truly wanted to change unfair laws.

2 managed

Artists managed to carve this special monument. It was not easy!

3 loaded

Before sailing, people loaded onto this swan boat. They piled on.

4 loveliest

Oregon's Crater Lake is one of the loveliest national parks. It is beautiful.

- Study each **Context Card**.
- Place the Vocabulary words in alphabetical order.

5 conversations

Conversations in a museum must be quiet. People should speak in whispers.

6 inspired

This statue has **inspired** people. It makes them believe in freedom.

7 reunion

This family went camping for their yearly **reunion**, or gathering.

8 currently

Currently, this fort is a museum. Soldiers no longer live here.

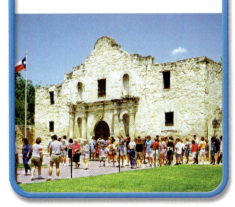

9 pleasure

People get **pleasure**, or enjoyment, from riding this old merry-go-round.

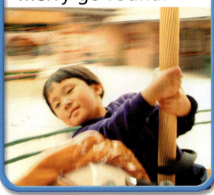

10 terror

When people look down at the Grand Canyon they may feel **terror**, or fear.

Background

✔ **TARGET VOCABULARY** **Traveling Now and Then** Are you ever **inspired** to travel? **Currently**, we travel easily by planes, trains, or cars. We can enjoy snacks and **conversations** flying 30,000 feet high! Long ago, people **managed** to travel, but it was difficult and often dangerous. Some travelers felt **terror** as they **loaded** onto horse-drawn wagons, camels, or creaky ships.

Travel today is fun and teaches us many new things. **Loveliest** of all, though, may be the **sincere pleasure** of coming home to a **reunion** with loved ones.

Travel Today	Travel Long Ago
Airplanes	Walking or horseback riding
Trains	Horse-drawn wagons
Cars and buses	Camels in caravan, or long line
Steam or gas-powered boat	Open boat or wind-powered ship
Interstate highways	Rough dirt roads or trails

People still use camels to travel, just as they did thousands of years ago!

Comprehension

TARGET SKILL **Sequence of Events**

As you read *The Journey of Oliver K. Woodman*, notice the sequence, or order, in which events take place. Use dates, times of day, and signal words to help you put the events in sequence on a chart like this one.

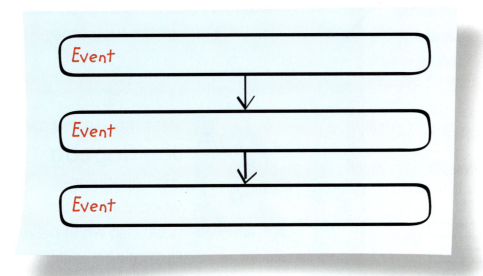

Event

Event

Event

✔ **TARGET STRATEGY** **Analyze/Evaluate**

The author uses letters to tell this story. What do you think of her choice to tell the story that way? Does it make story events easier or more difficult to follow? Does it make reading the story more or less enjoyable?

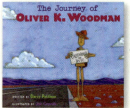

✓ TARGET VOCABULARY

sincere	inspired
managed	reunion
loaded	currently
loveliest	pleasure
conversations	terror

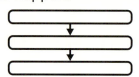

✓ TARGET SKILL

Sequence of Events
Tell the time order in which events happen.

✓ TARGET STRATEGY

Analyze/Evaluate Think about what you read. Then form an opinion about it.

GENRE

A **fantasy** is a story that could not happen in real life. As you read, ask yourself these questions: *Which details are realistic? Which are make-believe?*

MEET THE AUTHOR
Darcy Pattison

Oliver K. Woodman, the character Darcy Pattison created, has become so popular that students at schools in New York, Indiana, and other states have their own wooden models of him. Whenever they travel, they take Oliver with them and bring back photos and journal entries from his journey.

MEET THE ILLUSTRATOR
Joe Cepeda

Joe Cepeda does woodworking as a hobby, so when he was illustrating this story he drew Oliver K. Woodman as if he were really going to build the character out of wood. Author Darcy Pattison loves how Cepeda's art turned out. "Oliver has no mouth, yet you would swear that he's smiling at us," she says.

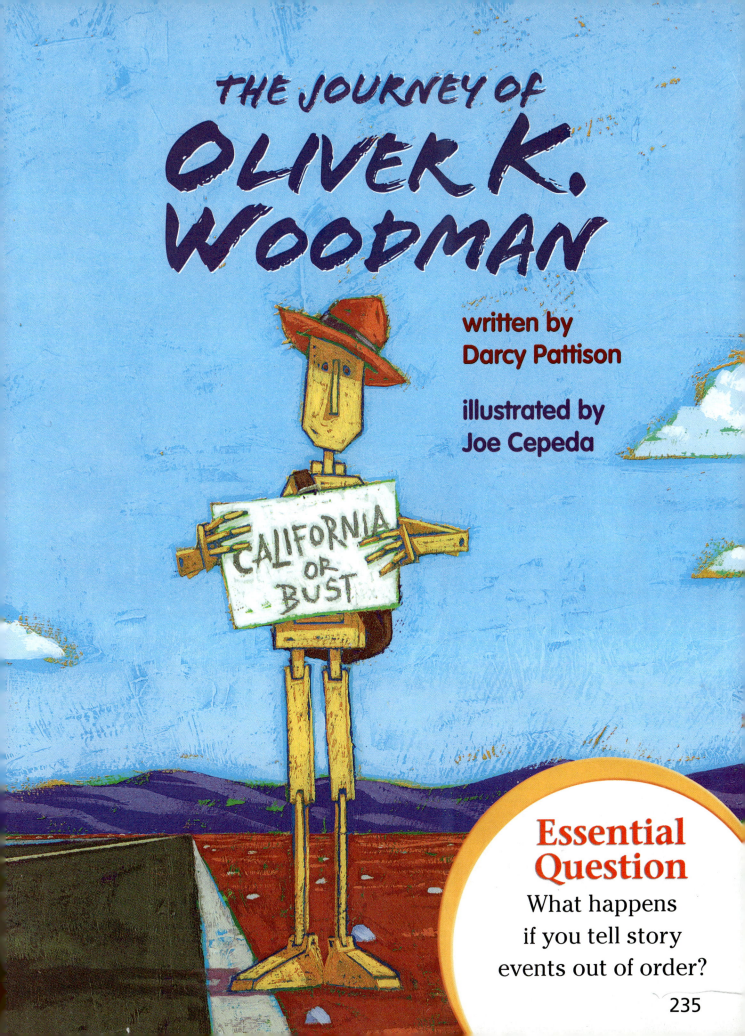

THE JOURNEY OF
OLIVER K. WOODMAN

written by
Darcy Pattison

illustrated by
Joe Cepeda

Essential Question

What happens if you tell story events out of order?

May 10
Redcrest, CA

Dear Uncle Ray,
    Please come to visit us this summer.
We will go camping. We can swim and
catch fish.
    You are my favorite uncle. Please say
you will come!

                    Love,
                    Tameka
                    XOXOXO

May 17
Rock Hill, SC

Dear Tameka,

I'd love to come to California, but I can't. I will be building kitchen cabinets for some new apartments all summer.

But maybe my friend Oliver will come to visit!

Love,
Uncle Ray

✓ STOP AND THINK

Sequence of Events Who wrote the first letter, Uncle Ray or Tameka? How can you figure this out?

237

Dear Traveler,

I am going to see Tameka Schwartz, 370 Park Avenue, Redcrest, California, 95569. Please give me a ride and help me get there. If you don't mind, drop a note to my friend Raymond Johnson, 111 Stony Lane, Rock Hill, South Carolina, 29730. He wants to keep up with my travels.

Thanks,
Oliver K. Woodman

June 1
Rock Hill, SC

Dear Favorite Niece Tameka,
Oliver left this morning. Let me know when
he gets there—it should take him a couple of
weeks. Or maybe more. It's hard to say.

Love,
Uncle Ray

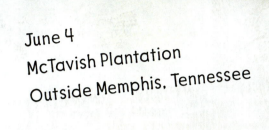

June 4
McTavish Plantation
Outside Memphis, Tennessee

Dear Ray:
    For two days, Oliver rode in the back of my truck and kept Bert, my Brahman bull, company. I delivered Bert to his new home and he's settling in, but he'll miss the late-night ==conversations== and singing with Oliver.
    I left Oliver east of the Mississippi River, just outside Memphis, and hurried home to my beloved Amelia.

            Yours truly,
            Jackson McTavish

June 8
Forrest City, AR

Hi! Mr. OK is OK. Quinn and Sherry went to a basketball game at The Pyramid in Memphis, Tennessee, last weekend and brought Mr. OK back. He hung out with us for a couple of days, and all the girls liked him better than Quinn. So when Quinn's cousin's boyfriend's aunt was leaving to visit her sick grandfather in Fort Smith, Arkansas, the guys loaded Mr. OK into the aunt's station wagon and sent him on his way. We didn't even get to say good-bye!

Raymond Johnson
111 Stony Lane
Rock Hill, SC 29730

Cherry (Sherry's sister),
for the Gang

P.S. If you see Mr. OK again, tell him we all said good-bye.

STOP AND THINK

Author's Craft How does Cherry's letter sound different from Jackson's letter on page 241? Which details make it sound this way?

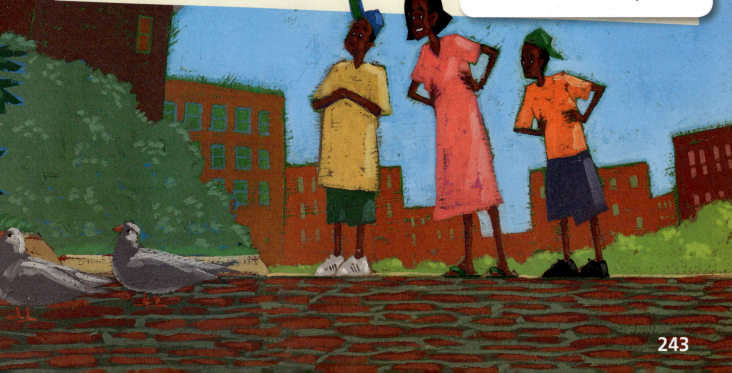

243

June 11
Albuquerque, NM

Hey, Ray—
I drive a moving van for Southeast Moving Company. I picked up Oliver at the Arkansas border, then drove west to Oklahoma City, Oklahoma, south to Dallas, Texas, northwest to Amarillo, Texas, east to Panhandle, Texas, then west again to Albuquerque, New Mexico.

He's an easy fella to travel with. He never needs bathroom stops. He doesn't care where we eat. And he stays awake with me all night. I'm sorry to see him go, but this week the company is sending me east, to Wauchula, Florida.

Trucking along—
Bobbi Jo

Raymond Johnson
111 Stony Lane
Rock Hill, SC 29730

June 28
Rock Hill, SC

Dear Tameka,
   I've had no word from Oliver in seventeen days.
I'm starting to worry. What if he is lost?
Please call me if he turns up at your house.

Love,
Uncle Ray

July 1
Redcrest, CA

Dear Uncle Ray,
No word from Oliver. Are you sure he's really coming?
I still wish we could see you. I asked Mama if we could come visit, but she said it costs too much. Daddy says he can't take off work that long. Ever since I asked, Mama keeps looking at family photo albums. When she sees your pictures, she says, "My baby brother!"

Love,
Tameka
XOXOXOX

July 4
Salt Lake City, UT

Dear Raymond Johnson:
My grandfather found Mr. Woodman in the middle of the reservation in New Mexico. Poor fella—a mouse was building a nest in his backpack. We don't know how he ended up way out there, and he's not telling.
Grandpa brought him to Utah to join me in the Fourth of July parade. I got so tired of smiling and waving at the crowds, but Mr. Woodman's brave smile ==inspired== me.
I just sent Mr. Woodman off with three sisters. They looked like such nice old ladies, so I know they'll take good care of him.

With all my love—
Melissa Tso, Miss Utah

P.S. I've enclosed an autographed picture.

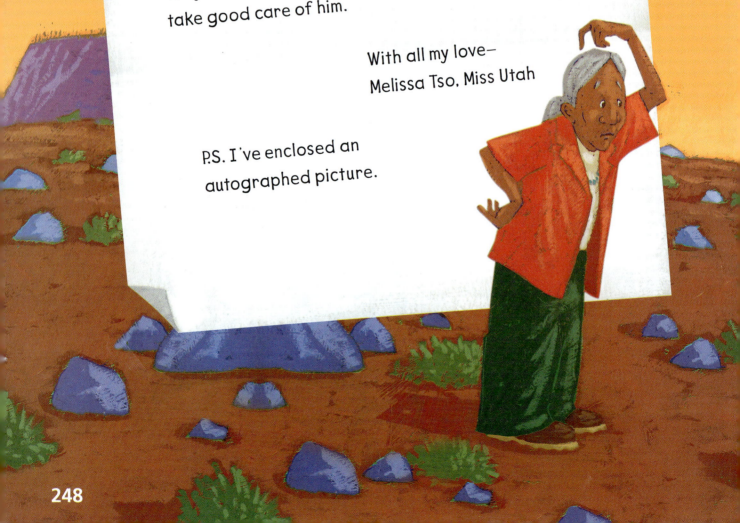

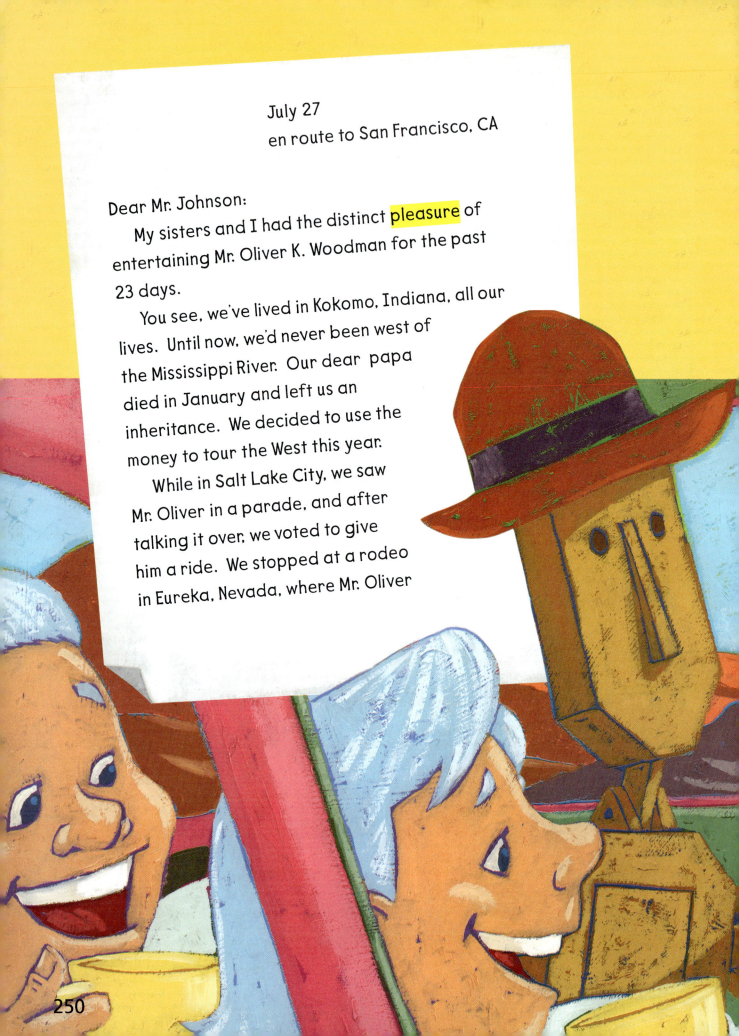

July 27
en route to San Francisco, CA

Dear Mr. Johnson:
My sisters and I had the distinct pleasure of entertaining Mr. Oliver K. Woodman for the past 23 days.

You see, we've lived in Kokomo, Indiana, all our lives. Until now, we'd never been west of the Mississippi River. Our dear papa died in January and left us an inheritance. We decided to use the money to tour the West this year.

While in Salt Lake City, we saw Mr. Oliver in a parade, and after talking it over, we voted to give him a ride. We stopped at a rodeo in Eureka, Nevada, where Mr. Oliver

met an old friend named Bert. They had a moving reunion.

We are heading south to San Francisco to see the Golden Gate Bridge, so we left Mr. Oliver yesterday in Rough and Ready, California. He should be at Miss Tameka's soon.

The Claremont Sisters
Agnes, Maggie, and Lucinda

P.S. We had afternoon tea every day. Mr. Oliver has the loveliest manners.

July 28
To: Raymond Johnson
Re: Mr. Oliver K. Woodman

Our family, <mark>currently</mark> on vacation, picked up the above-named person in what I thought was a misguided goodwill gesture. Little did I know how lucky that gesture would be.

Last night, we pitched tents in the Redwood forest. I woke at 3:00 A.M. to screams of <mark>terror</mark>. Bears! Your friend <mark>managed</mark> to frighten them away. He saved our lives.

With the deepest and most <mark>sincere</mark> gratitude, we intend to deliver him to the doorstep of Tameka Schwartz within the next two days.

Gratefully yours,
Bernard Grape,
Attorney-at-Law

Raymond Johnson
111 Stony Lane
Rock Hill, SC
29730

STOP AND THINK

Analyze/Evaluate Why do you think the author decided to tell the story with letters?

August 1
Redcrest, CA

Dear Uncle Ray,

Guess who came to dinner? Oliver! He is so much fun! We are camping in the backyard tonight. I hear he's not scared of anything, so I'm glad he'll be there. Tomorrow, at the river, I'll let him hold my fishing pole while I swim.

Guess what else? Daddy and Mama talked it over. We're coming to your house next month, and we'll bring Oliver home. Isn't it wonderful?

Love,
Tameka
XOXOXOX

P.S. Knock, knock. Who's there? Olive. Olive who? Olive both you and Oliver!

Oliver's Journey

TICKER-TAPE PARADE FOR HOMETOWN BOY

by Demetrius Dickson

Oliver K. Woodman will return home today amid national acclaim for his cross-country journey. Woodman began his trip on June 1, in Rock Hill, South Carolina, and arrived in Redcrest, California, on August 1.

The Rock Hill City Council announced that a ticker-tape parade to honor Woodman will be held today at 10:00 A.M., starting at the corner of Main Street and Cherry Road and proceeding down Cherry Road to Cherry Park.

Raymond Johnson and Tameka Schwartz, friends of Mr. Woodman, will host a picnic in his honor at Cherry Park at noon. At 1:00 P.M., Mr. Woodman will show postcards and mementos from his trip. The public is invited.

Your Turn

Traveling Tales

Write a Journal Entry
Imagine that you are Oliver K. Woodman. Write a journal entry about how you ended up in the middle of a reservation in New Mexico. What happened there?

LANGUAGE ARTS

On the Road

Plan a Trip If you could take a cross-country trip, what places would you want to see? With a partner, use a map of the United States to plan a trip. Decide which states you will travel through. Make a list of the places you will visit. PARTNERS

First Things First

Turn and Talk Was it easy or hard to follow the order of events in *The Journey of Oliver K. Woodman*? With a partner, discuss what features in the story helped you keep track of places and dates. How would the story have been different if events were not told in order? SEQUENCE OF EVENTS

Social Studies

Moving the U.S. Mail

✓ TARGET VOCABULARY

sincere	inspired
managed	reunion
loaded	currently
loveliest	pleasure
conversations	terror

GENRE

Informational text gives factual information about a topic. This is an online encyclopedia.

TEXT FOCUS

A **timeline** is a line that shows the order in which events happened. Discuss the timeline shown here.
Try to figure out the year each form of transportation was used by the United States Postal Service.

 **File   Edit   View   Favorites**

Moving the U.S. Mail

The United States Postal Service

The United States Postal Service has changed over the years. In colonial times, all kinds of people helped deliver mail. Sometimes letters ==managed== to get through. Sometimes they didn't.

Delivery Times
New York to San Francisco

1800

Pony Express 13–14 days by train to Missouri, then on horseback

Getting mail brings <mark>pleasure</mark> to many, but it has never been easy to deliver. Today the Postal Service makes a <mark>sincere</mark> effort to deliver all mail. <mark>Currently</mark> it delivers hundreds of millions of messages daily.

Transportation Changes

Having <mark>conversations</mark> by mail has gotten much faster. Why is this? Transportation has improved. Long ago, people carried mail on foot, horseback, and stagecoaches. Today's mail is <mark>loaded</mark> onto trucks and planes.

In 1775 Benjamin Franklin became the first Postmaster General.

1900   **2000**

Transcontinental Railroad 7 days

Airplane 6–7 hours

File   Edit   View   Favorites   Tools   Help

Golden Moments of Mail History

Gold was discovered in California in 1848. People rushed west. The California Gold Rush ==inspired== faster mail delivery. It would be a long time until they could have a ==reunion== with their families, so gold seekers wanted mail from home.

Pony Express riders carried mail to California in 1860 and 1861. Their rides could be full of ==terror==. They faced blizzards and bandits.

By 1869 the Transcontinental Railroad linked railroads in the east with California. The mail moved faster than ever.

A Postmark from the Heart

Each year around February 14, mail from around the world takes a detour. This mail isn't slowed by blizzards or bandits—it's delayed by love! In honor of Valentine's Day, cards are mailed to the small town of Valentine, Texas. They get the town's postmark and go on to their final destination.

Each year, in Valentine, Texas, the school holds a design contest. The city council chooses the ==loveliest== design to be used as that year's postmark.

Aunt Susie
123 Msososo Street
Austin, TX 12307

Making Connections

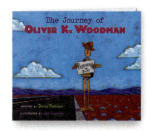

Text to Self

Write a Letter What would you do with Oliver K. Woodman if he visited you? Write a letter to Uncle Ray about the adventures you would have. Include a date, greeting, and closing. Use friendly, informal language.

Text to Text

Compare and Contrast What if Oliver had traveled to California by Pony Express? Would his trip be shorter or longer? How else would it be similar to or different from his travels in *The Journey of Oliver K. Woodman*? Use information from "Moving the U.S. Mail" to help you write a paragraph about Oliver's trip by Pony Express.

Text to World

Connect to Social Studies Use a road map of the United States to find the places that Oliver K. Woodman visited. Identify the general direction in which he traveled.

Grammar

Abbreviations An **abbreviation** is a short way to write a word. Most abbreviations begin with a capital letter and end with a period.

Academic Language

abbreviation

Some Common Abbreviations					
Months	February	Feb.	April	Apr.	October	Oct.
	March	Mar.	August	Aug.	December	Dec.
Days	Saturday	Sat.	Monday	Mon.	Wednesday	Wed.
	Sunday	Sun.	Tuesday	Tues.	Thursday	Thurs.
Addresses	Street	St.	Road	Rd.	Avenue	Ave.

 **Write the abbreviation for each day, month, or street name below.**

❶ Saturday

❷ December

❸ Avenue

❹ March 28

❺ 325 Elm Road

❻ Wednesday, August 6, 1999

❼ November 3

❽ 932 Swanton Street

Conventions You can use abbreviations for the titles of people in many kinds of writing. Usually, you abbreviate the names of days, months, and kinds of streets only in addresses and lists.

Incorrect	Correct
mon., jan 6 Baseball Card Club meets at mrs Joy Cho's home 222 Allen st	Mon., Jan. 6 Baseball Card Club meets at Mrs. Joy Cho's home 222 Allen St.
wed, feb 11 Stamp Club Dinner at the home of dr Calvin Cook 1740 Parker ave	Wed., Feb. 11 Stamp Club Dinner at the home of Dr. Calvin Cook 1740 Parker Ave.

Connect Grammar to Writing

As you edit your dialogue, check to make sure you have used capital letters, commas, and periods correctly.

Write to Express

✔ **Voice** In *The Journey of Oliver K. Woodman*, you can tell how Tameka feels when she says in a letter, "You are my favorite uncle. Please say you will come!" As you revise your **dialogue**, be sure your characters speak in a way that shows their feelings.

Ava wrote about two girls who find a cave. When Ava revised her draft, her changes showed the girls' feelings.

Writing Traits Checklist

✔ **Ideas**
Is my dialogue interesting?

✔ **Organization**
Can my readers tell what is happening?

✔ **Word Choice**
Did I use formal or informal words that suit my characters?

✔ **Voice**
Do my characters' feelings show?

✔ **Sentence Fluency**
Did I use different kinds of sentences?

✔ **Conventions**
Did I indent each paragraph?

Revised Draft

Mia and Jade were exploring the woods behind their new house. "Hey, ~~I found something,~~ look at this!" whispered said Mia.

"Wow, It's a cave!" said Jade. "Let's go in."

"Are you kidding?"
~~No, I don't want to.~~

"Why not?"

"There could be bears in there!"

Jade smiled. "Don't be silly. ~~I don't think so.~~"

The Cave

by Ava Garcia

Mia and Jade were exploring the woods behind their new house. "Hey, look at this!" whispered Mia.

"Wow, a cave!" said Jade. "Let's go in."

"Are you kidding?"

"Why not?"

"There could be bears in there!"

Jade smiled. "Don't be silly. Mrs. Chen said there are no bears around here."

Mia said, "Well, I have a cold, and Dr. David says damp places are bad for colds."

"You're just scared. I'm going in. I bet there's something fantastic in there."

"Well...okay. Let's go," said Mia.

> I added words that show my characters' feelings. I also made sure to write abbreviations correctly.

Reading as a Writer

Which parts let you really hear how each girl feels? Where can you show your own characters' feelings more clearly?

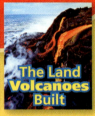

voyage

lava

rippled

arrival

guided

twisted

aboard

anchor

spotted

bay

Vocabulary Reader

Context Cards

Vocabulary in Context

1 **voyage**

The explorer's **voyage**, or ocean trip, to Hawaii took more than a year.

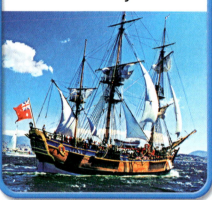

2 **lava**

Hawaii's islands formed from **lava**, or hot melted rock, from volcanoes.

3 **rippled**

This lava in Hawaii **rippled** into tiny black waves as it cooled.

4 **arrival**

When visitors first come to Hawaii, their **arrival** is welcomed.

- **Study each Context Card.**
- **Tell a story about two or more pictures, using their Vocabulary words.**

5 guided

This man guided, or led, tourists through a park in Hawaii.

6 twisted

These girls twisted wire around flowers to attach them to crowns.

7 aboard

Each racing canoe has six people aboard. They are seated in the boat.

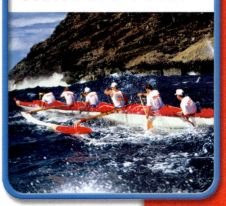

8 anchor

A heavy anchor holds this boat in place when the boat is stopped.

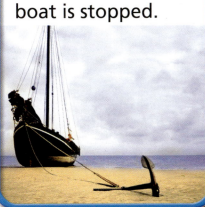

9 spotted

Whales can be spotted, or seen, in the ocean near Hawaii.

10 bay

People can swim, snorkel, or sail in the gentle waters of this bay, or inlet.

Background

Seals at Play When aboard a ship for an ocean voyage, it's fun to look for seals. Seals are playful creatures. They can easily be spotted looking for supper in deep water rippled with fish. They also love splashing around in the shallow water of a harbor or a bay.

To a seal, the arrival of a new boat means a chance to make new friends. After the boat has been guided into port and the anchor lowered, the seals gather, showing off with tricks. They hope to earn a tasty treat as a reward.

Monk seals in Hawaii like sunbathing on rocks formed from cooled lava. Sadly, they are at risk of dying out. Some monk seals get twisted and tangled in fishing nets.

Comprehension

Author's Purpose

As you read *Dog-of-the-Sea-Waves*, think about the words and ideas the author uses to describe Hawaii. Write these details on a chart like this one. Then use the details to help you figure out the author's purpose, or reason, for writing the story.

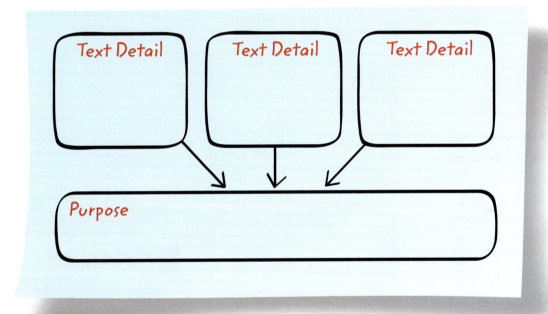

Text Detail

Text Detail

Text Detail

Purpose

✔ TARGET STRATEGY **Question**

As you read, ask yourself, *What does the author want you to learn from the selection?* Details from the story can help you answer the question.

Dog-of-the-Sea-Waves
in English & Hawaiian
by James Rumford

✔ **TARGET VOCABULARY**

voyage	twisted
lava	aboard
rippled	anchor
arrival	spotted
guided	bay

✔ **TARGET SKILL**

Author's Purpose Use text details to tell why an author writes a book. State in your own words the author's theme, or message, about Hawaii.

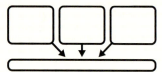

✔ **TARGET STRATEGY**

Question Ask questions before you read, while you read, and after you read.

GENRE

Realistic fiction is a story with events that could happen in real life.

MEET THE AUTHOR AND ILLUSTRATOR

James Rumford

A longtime resident of Hawaii, James Rumford hopes his readers will learn *aloha 'aina,* or "to cherish these special islands," as much as he does. Scattered throughout the pages of *Dog-of-the-Sea-Waves* are tiny drawings of plants and animals that are found in Hawaii. Many of them are at risk of dying out. Rumford included these to show that Hawaii's natural beauty needs our protection.

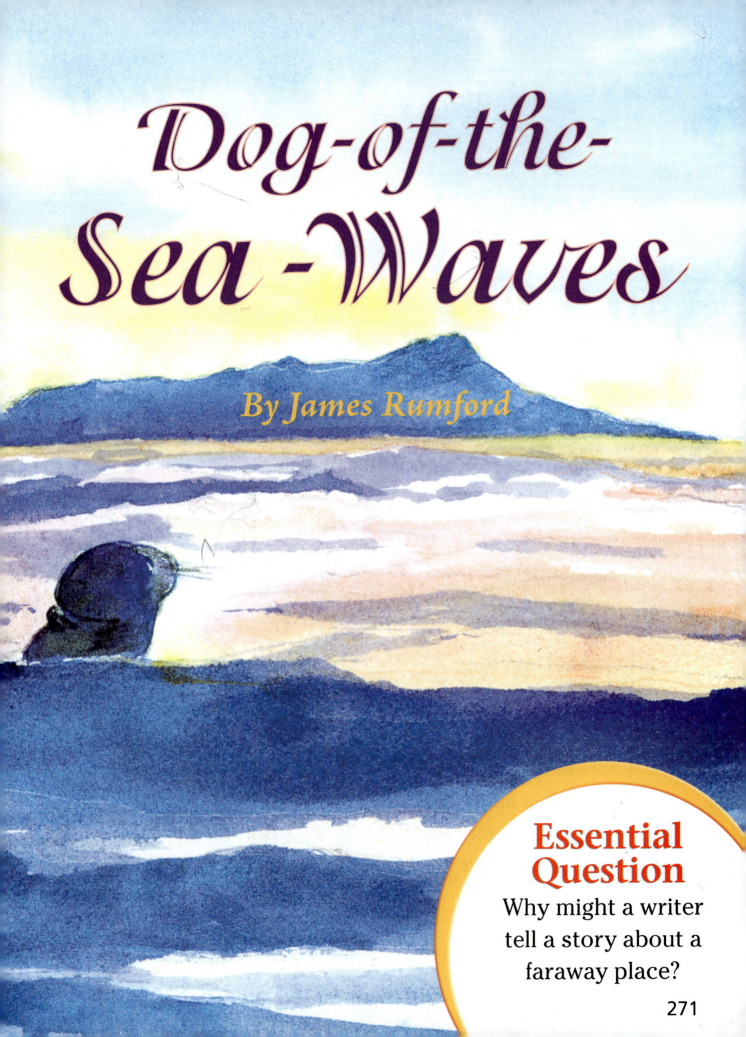

Dog-of-the-Sea-Waves

By James Rumford

Five brothers explore the Hawaiian Islands. Manu, the youngest brother, saves the life of an injured seal and the two become friends. When it's time for the brothers to go home, Manu is unsure if he'll ever see his friend again.

O'ahu Tree Snail

In the days when the sun, the moon, and the stars <mark>guided</mark> birds with seeds in their bellies to these islands, when ocean waves brought driftwood teeming with life, when storms brought frightened birds in the clouds and insects on the wind, the Hawaiian Islands grew green and lush.

The streams and lagoons <mark>rippled</mark> with fish. And the forests flashed with the feathers of birds and the rainbow wings of insects.

Belted Wrasse

The Hawaiian Islands welcomed all life that made the long, long journey to its shores, and some two thousand years ago, they embraced the first people to come.

In those days of first canoes, first footprints, first campfires, there were five brothers who came from their home far to the south to explore these islands. They were Hōkū, who loved the stars, Nāʻale, who loved the sea, ʻŌpua, who loved clouds, Makani, who loved the wind, and Manu, who loved birds.

Kamehameha Butterfly

One night, soon after their ==arrival==, Hōkū said, "See, my brothers, that new star I've discovered? It always points north!"

Everyone except Manu looked up at the sparkling North Star. Everyone except Manu began talking excitedly about all the other new things they had discovered.

"New things!" Manu exclaimed. "I miss the old things. Where are the coconuts, the bananas, the sweet potatoes? And how about the pigs, the chickens, the dogs?"

"We'll go home and bring these things back here with us," said Hōkū.

"We're coming back?" Manu cried. "I don't want to come back. I just want to go home."

But home was a long ocean ==voyage== away, and there was much to do before they could leave—food and water to gather and sails to repair. So no one spoke.

The next day, as the brothers were exploring a lagoon, Manu <mark>spotted</mark> an animal lying at the water's edge.

"It's a dog, my brothers! A dog!"

At last! Something familiar in this strange land.

But when they got close, they saw that it was like no dog they had ever seen before. It had flippers for legs, a fish's tail, and the body of a dolphin. And it was badly hurt.

Manu tried to calm the animal. He brought cool water and cleaned the wound. He built a shelter against the sun and kept the fur wet with seawater.

The brothers left Manu. They had no time for an animal that was going to die. They had to prepare for the long sea voyage home.

STOP AND THINK

Question What kind of animal have the brothers found? Why does Manu help it? What do you think will happen if the animal lives?

But the animal didn't die.

"I will call you 'Dog-of-the-Sea-Waves,'" Manu said on the third day, as he fed him fish.

At the end of the week, the two had their first swim together, and before long, they were playing tag in the waves. Manu made up a silly chant:

Dog-of-the-Sea-Waves,
Dog-with-no-paws,
Dog-with-no-ears,
Dog-with-no-wag,
We're friends!

Granulated Cowry

Manu giggled, and Dog-of-the-Sea-Waves tickled his cheek with his whiskers.

"Come help me dry berries and roots for the voyage home," called Hōkū.

"We need fish," scolded Nāʻale.

"There's water to gather," scowled ʻŌpua.

"And sails to repair," cried Makani.

But Manu pretended not to hear. Instead he and Dog-of-the-Sea-Waves played together and got into all kinds of trouble. They terrorized the fish Nāʻale was trying to catch. They made a mess of the beach where Hōkū was drying food. They played with Makani's ropes and accidentally pulled ʻŌpua's gourds off the boat, tripping Makani, who fell into the water.

No one laughed. The two were separated, and Manu was put to work.

Manu gathered berries for Hōkū. He caught fish for Nā'ale. He fetched water for 'Ōpua. He **twisted** rope for Makani. But every evening after his work was done, he slipped off to meet his friend, and they played in the waves until it got too dark to see. Then Manu swam ashore, and Dog-of-the-Sea-Waves went hunting for food.

After many months of hard work, the boat was finally ready to leave. At the last moment, Manu dived into the water to say goodbye to Dog-of-the-Sea-Waves. As the brothers yelled for Manu to get **aboard**, Dog-of-the-Sea-Waves brushed his whiskers against Manu's cheek, then disappeared beneath the waves.

Hawaiian Raspberry

The brothers sailed down the island chain. When they came to the last island, 'Ōpua said, "Is that a cloud on the side of that mountain, or smoke? Let's go see."

Curious, the brothers anchored their boat in a quiet ==bay== and swam ashore.

Halfway up the mountain, Makani felt a warm wind and hesitated. But his brothers told him not to worry.

After a few more steps, Manu noticed that the birds were silent. But his brothers paid no attention.

Then—a jolt!

The earth heaved up and slammed the brothers to the ground. Deep cracks appeared, then flames.

Hōkū grabbed Manu's hand, and the brothers fled down the slope. But a river of fire cut them off from the sea and forced them to the cliffs.

The earth shuddered, and the five brothers jumped—into the sea far below.

Wekiu Bug

281

But the sea they landed in was a monster. It thrashed from the earthquakes. It hissed from the burning lava. It lashed out at the brothers and grabbed Manu. In an instant, he was gone.

Makani filled his lungs with air and went to the very depths of the ocean, but there was no sign of Manu. ʻŌpua, with his voice like thunder, shouted for Manu above the crashing waves, but there was no answer. Nāʻale, who loved the sea, begged it to be calm, but it wouldn't listen.

Dragon Moray

STOP AND THINK

Author's Craft What comparison does the author make to create a picture in your mind of how the sea looked, felt, and sounded?

All this time, Manu was fighting to get to the surface, but the sea wouldn't let go. Then he felt the whiskers. Manu clasped his arms around Dog-of-the-Sea-Waves, and up they went.

Pompom Crab

It was Hōkū who spotted them. The brothers raced toward Manu and cradled him above the waves.

"Manu, Manu," they cried over and over as they made their way to the boat. And to Dog-of-the-Sea-Waves they chanted their thanks:

Dog-that-swims-the-depths,
Dog-that-braves-the-currents,
Dog-that-knows-the-sea,
Dog-that-cares-for-our-brother.

The brothers then weighed <mark>anchor</mark> and headed for the southern sea and home. Manu stood on the deck and listened to Dog-of-the-Sea-Waves barking goodbye.

"We'll be back," Manu shouted.

Happyface Spider

And when they returned, they came with their families. They embraced the land and made it their home.

 STOP AND THINK

Author's Purpose Tell in your own words what you think the author wants readers to learn from the brothers' story.

Your Turn

Loving Nature

Write About Nature
Each of the brothers in *Dog-of-the-Sea-Waves* loved a different part of nature. What is your favorite part of nature? Why? Write about it.
PERSONAL RESPONSE

> My favorite part of nature is the way the leaves change color in the fall.

Sing Along

Create a Chant Manu and his brothers make up two chants. One chant is a silly one, and the other is a thankful one. In a group, make up your own chants about an animal. Perform them for the class. SMALL GROUP

Faraway Lands

Turn and Talk With a partner, discuss the things you learned in *Dog-of-the-Sea-Waves.* What did you learn about friendships between people and animals? What did you learn about Hawaii? Why do you think the author wrote the story?
AUTHOR'S PURPOSE

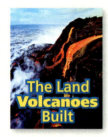

The Land
Volcanoes
Built

GENRE

Informational text gives factual information about a topic. This is a magazine article.

TEXT FOCUS

A **diagram** is a drawing that shows how something works. Examine the diagram on page 289. Then explain to a partner the steps that lead to a volcanic eruption.

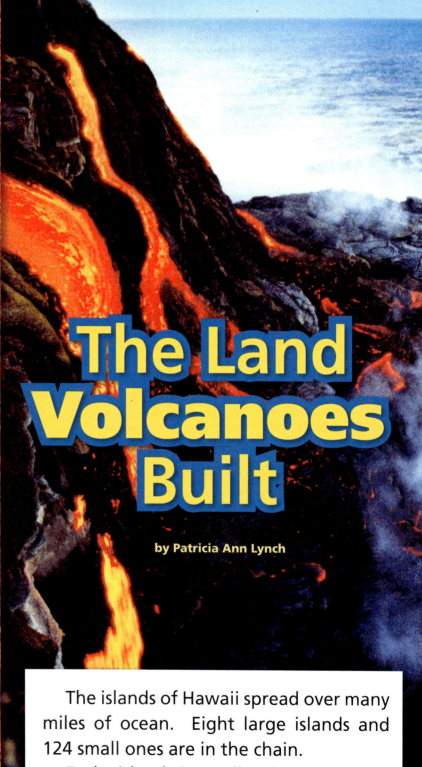

The Land Volcanoes Built

by Patricia Ann Lynch

The islands of Hawaii spread over many miles of ocean. Eight large islands and 124 small ones are in the chain.

Each island is really the top of a mountain that pokes out of the sea. How were these islands formed? The answer is *volcanoes*.

What Is a Volcano?

A volcano is an opening, or vent, that goes deep into Earth. Deep within Earth it is so hot that rock melts. The melted rock is called magma.

Sometimes magma is pushed up and pours out of the volcano. Then the magma is called <mark>lava</mark>. The lava cools and hardens. It builds up. Over time, it can form a tall mountain. Each of the Hawaiian Islands formed in this way.

A Volcano Erupts

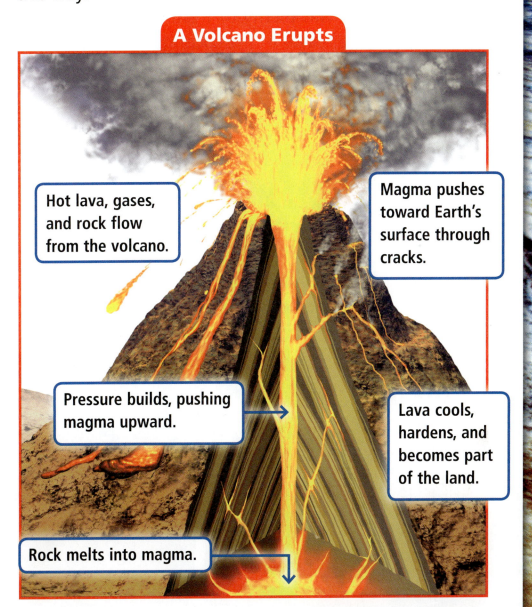

Hot lava, gases, and rock flow from the volcano.

Magma pushes toward Earth's surface through cracks.

Pressure builds, pushing magma upward.

Lava cools, hardens, and becomes part of the land.

Rock melts into magma.

Life Arrives

At first, the islands were bare. Waves ==rippled== on empty shores. Life came much later. Wind and water carried plant seeds. Sea animals such as monk seals swam there. Other animals made the ==voyage aboard== objects floating in the sea. The ==arrival== of birds brought song.

The first people paddled in canoes from other islands. The stars ==guided== them across the Pacific Ocean. The travelers ==spotted== the islands. They dropped ==anchor== in a calm ==bay== and came ashore. The new islands were good places to live. There was plenty of fresh water to drink and lots of food. The leaves of the coconut tree could be used to build thatched shelters. Coconut husks could be ==twisted== into strong ropes. These people became the first Hawaiians.

People from China, Japan, Samoa, the Philippines, and other countries live in Hawaii today.

Making Connections

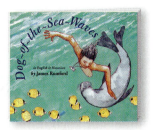

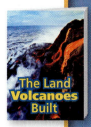

Text to Self

Draw a Picture Imagine you are a brother in *Dog-of-the-Sea-Waves*. Draw a picture of what you might see when you arrive at one of the islands. Use the text and pictures from *Dog-of-the-Sea-Waves* and "The Land Volcanoes Built" for ideas.

Text to Text

Connect to Science Find sections in *Dog-of-the-Sea-Waves* that refer to volcanoes or their effects. Use what you learned in "The Land Volcanoes Built" to explain to a partner what was really happening during that passage.

Text to World

Volcano Hunt Besides Hawaii, where are volcanoes found around the world? Do research on the Internet or in reference books. Share your findings with the class.

Grammar

What Is an Adverb? An adverb is a word that describes a verb. Adverbs can tell *how, when,* or *where* an action happens. Adverbs can come before or after the verbs they describe.

Kim saw a seal at the zoo **yesterday**. (tells *when*)

She **carefully** touched the seal's belly. (tells *how*)

The seal eats **there**. (tells *where*)

It barked **loudly**. (tells *how*)

Turn and Talk **Work with a partner. Read the sentences aloud. Find the adverb in each sentence.**

1. Alex ran ahead.

2. He reached the beach first.

3. He eagerly searched for the seal.

4. He looked everywhere for his friend.

5. Alex found the seal playing quietly in the ocean.

292

Sentence Fluency Short, choppy sentences can be combined to make your writing smoother. Combine two sentences by moving an adverb. Often you can choose where to place the adverb in the new sentence.

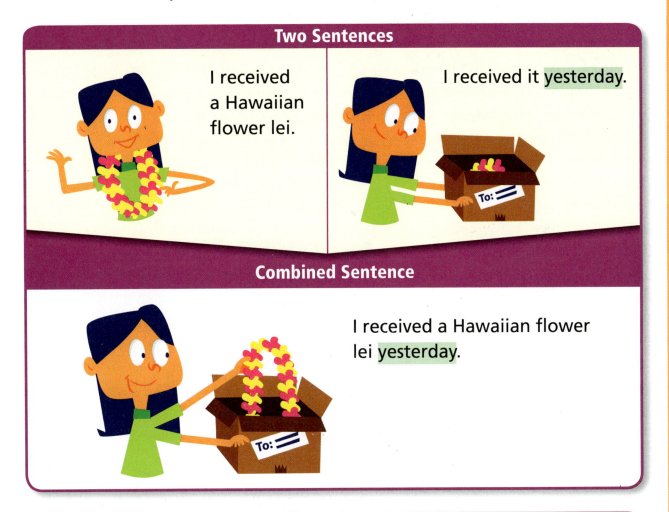

Two sentences:	A lei should be draped over the shoulders. A lei should be draped gently.
Combined sentence:	A lei should be draped gently over the shoulders.

Connect Grammar to Writing

As you revise your story next week, think about combining sentences by moving an adverb.

Write to Express

☑ **Ideas** Once you have chosen a topic for a story, or **fictional narrative**, explore your topic. Think about it and fill a page with ideas.

Louis decided to write a story about pioneers. He began by listing details about his characters, setting, and plot. Then he made a story map and added even more details.

Writing Process Checklist

▶ **Prewriting**

☑ **Did I pick a topic that my audience and I will enjoy?**

☑ **Did I decide what my characters and setting are like?**

☑ **Did I plan a good beginning, middle, and end?**

☑ **Did I think of enough details?**

Drafting

Revising

Proofreading

Publishing

Exploring a Topic

Who? a family in a covered wagon
mother, father, son

Where and when? a desert
about 1850

What? get stuck in a sandstorm
water supply running low

Story Map

Setting	Characters
the desert, during a sandstorm inside a covered wagon, hot, crowded with furniture	Sam: scared, tired of waiting Ma: hopeful Pop: calm, cheerful, good storyteller

Plot

Beginning Sam and his family have been stuck in a sandstorm for ten hours.

Middle Sam is hot, scared that they will run out of water.

Pop tells him not to worry. Ma talks about their new home out West.

End Pop tells Sam a story.

Pop's story helps Sam relax until the storm ends.

> When I organized my fictional narrative, I added more details.

Reading as a Writer

Which of Louis's details help you picture what is happening? What details can you add to your own chart to make the plot clear?

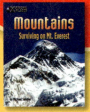

✓ **TARGET VOCABULARY**

approached

section

avalanches

increases

equipment

tanks

slopes

altitude

succeed

halt

Vocabulary Reader

Context Cards

Vocabulary in Context

1 approached

Climbers approached this mountain from the west. Slowly, they got nearer to it.

2 section

The top section, or part, of this mountain is the steepest.

3 avalanches

When avalanches occur, the powerful sliding snow can knock trees down.

4 increases

When storms blow in, the danger to climbers increases, or becomes greater.

- Study each **Context Card**.
- Ask a question that uses one of the Vocabulary words.

5 **equipment**

Mountain climbers check their supplies, or **equipment**, before a climb.

6 **tanks**

Tanks that hold oxygen help climbers breathe in the high, thin air.

7 **slopes**

Gentle **slopes** near the bottom of the mountain are easiest to climb.

8 **altitude**

The **altitude**, or height, of Granite Peak in Montana is 12,799 feet high.

9 **succeed**

Everyone's goal is to reach the summit. If climbers plan well, they will **succeed**!

10 **halt**

Climbers come to a **halt** when it gets dark. They stop for the night.

Background

Mountain Climbing Mountain peaks may look beautiful from far away, but they can also be deadly. Climbers should prepare long before the slopes are approached. Improper equipment increases the chances of a climb coming to a dangerous halt.

Smart climbers use maps showing each section of the mountain. They may also require special safety equipment to survive avalanches. Oxygen tanks for breathing at high altitude may also be needed. Climbers who have planned well are most likely to succeed!

helmet

ice ax

ice anchor

rope

windbreaker

harness

backpack

carabiner

boots with crampons

snow pants

Comprehension

Text and Graphic Features

As you read *Mountains: Surviving on Mt. Everest*, pay attention to the text, charts, and other graphic features the author uses to help make the information clear. Use a chart like this one to list the text and graphic features in this selection. Tell why you think the author uses them.

Text or Graphic Feature	Page	Purpose

✓ **TARGET STRATEGY** **Infer/Predict**

Text and graphic features, such as headings, captions, and charts, can help you predict which details are more important to the selection. Look at the text and graphic features to predict what the author considers important.

Main Selection

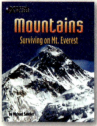

✔ TARGET VOCABULARY

approached	tanks
section	slopes
avalanches	altitude
increases	succeed
equipment	halt

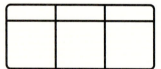
✔ TARGET SKILL

Text and Graphic Features Tell how words and photos work together.

✔ TARGET STRATEGY

Infer/Predict Use text and graphic clues to figure out more about the selection.

GENRE
Informational text gives factual information about a topic.

MEET THE AUTHOR
Michael Sandler

Michael Sandler enjoys extreme adventures. He loves to travel and has been to the foothills of Mount Everest, the highest mountain in the world. Several years ago while touring Africa, he got lost in the Sahara, the world's largest desert. That adventure might have helped him later to write *Deserts: Surviving in the Sahara*.

Other extreme books by Sandler include *Oceans: Surviving in the Deep Sea* and *Rain Forests: Surviving in the Amazon*.

Mountains
Surviving on Mt. Everest

by Michael Sandler

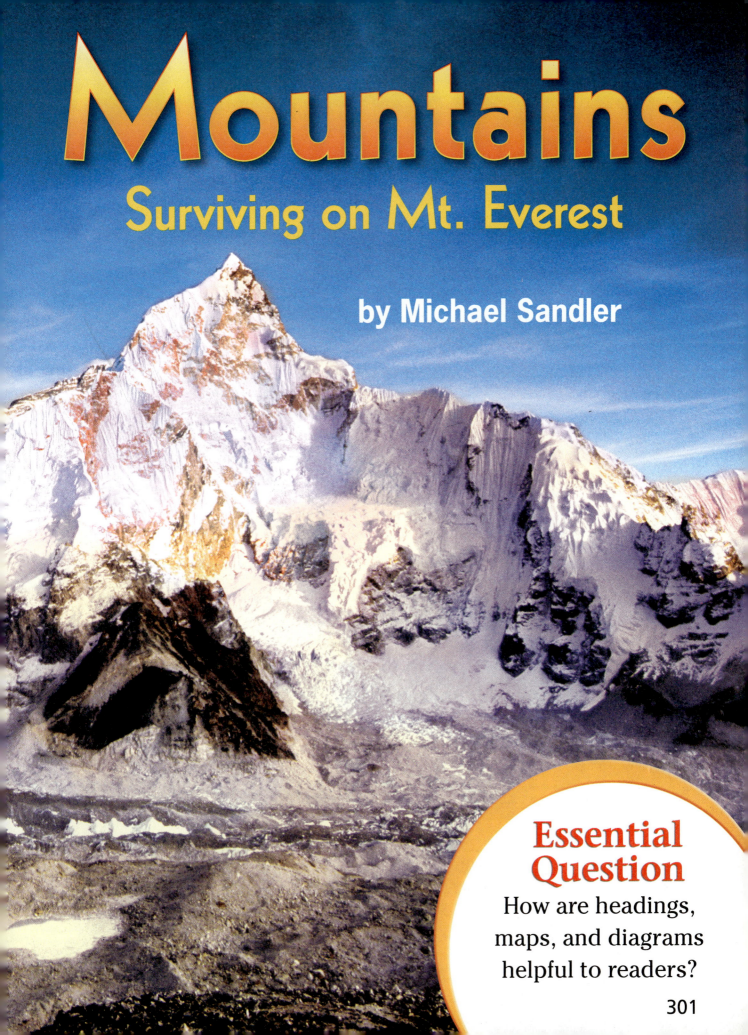

Essential Question

How are headings, maps, and diagrams helpful to readers?

Climbing Mount Everest

The clock showed almost midnight. The temperature was freezing. Icy winds roared by.

A group of people huddled in the darkness on a rocky ridge. In moments, they would begin the final stage of a dangerous journey. They were climbing to the top of Mount Everest, the world's highest mountain.

Among the climbers was Temba Tsheri (SHUHR ee)
Sherpa. Just two weeks before, Temba had celebrated his
16th birthday. Now he was trying to survive in one of the
world's most extreme places. Making it to the top of Everest
was Temba's dream. He would be the youngest person ever to
reach the summit, which is 29,035 feet (8,850 meters) high.

What Are Mountains?

Mountains are a type of tall landform. They rise high above the area around them. Mountains are taller than hills. They can rise thousands of feet (kilometers) in the air. They are found all over the world, even beneath the sea.

A group of mountains is called a range. The biggest mountain range in North America is the Rocky Mountains. The Andes (AN deez), in South America, is the world's longest mountain range.

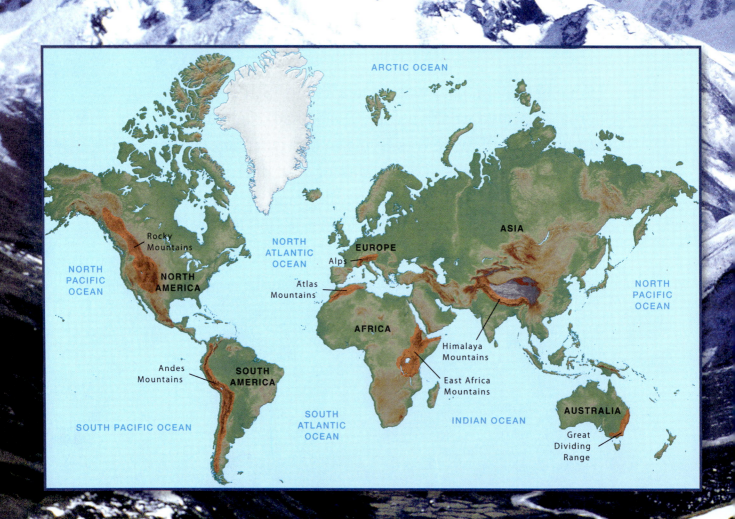

Mount Everest, the mountain Temba was climbing, is part of the Himalaya (hihm uh LAY uh) Mountains. The name "Himalaya" means "home of snow." This Asian range is the world's highest. It includes nine of the ten tallest mountains on Earth.

Mountains cover one quarter of Earth's land surface.

Mountain Conditions

As Temba approached Everest's summit, survival became harder and harder. Mountain conditions get more extreme the higher a person climbs.

Air contains less and less oxygen as the altitude increases. Breathing becomes nearly impossible. Thin air can cause headaches and dizziness at 10,000 feet (3,048 meters). Higher up, it can be deadly.

Humans cannot survive for long at the top section of mountains like Everest. Hurricane-force winds can reach 130 miles per hour (209 kph). Temperatures can plummet to –100F (–73C) during the night. Blowing snow makes it hard to see. Temba was headed here.

Frostbite can happen when it's so cold that hands, feet, and other parts of the body freeze solid. Frostbite can cause people to lose fingers, toes— even their noses.

Why Do People Climb Mountains?

People climb mountains for many reasons. Some enjoy the thrill of being high above the clouds. Others like the challenge of testing their skills.

For decades, however, reaching the top of Everest was a test that no climber could pass. The first attempts to climb Everest were made during the 1920s. Again and again, the climbing teams stopped short of their goal. Avalanches, storms, sickness, and exhaustion brought them to a halt.

Then, in 1953, two climbers finally succeeded— Sir Edmund Hillary and Tenzing Norgay. Sir Hillary was from New Zealand. Norgay was a Sherpa from Nepal (nuh PAWL).

Temba had tried to climb Everest before. It ended, however, in failure.

> ✔️ **STOP AND THINK**
>
> **Text and Graphic Features** These pages include headings, a caption, and a boxed fact. What kinds of information do these text features provide?

Sir Edmund Hillary (left) and Tenzing Norgay (right) show off their survival equipment in 1953.

Temba's Mistake

"I didn't have enough training or proper <mark>equipment</mark>," Temba said. He was almost at the summit when his oxygen supply ran out.

Without oxygen, Temba couldn't think clearly. He made a terrible mistake. He took off his gloves to tie his boots. His fingers froze. Temba suffered frostbite on both hands. He had to turn back just 70 feet (21 meters) from his goal.

The next time around, however, Temba was prepared. He had trained hard. He had the right equipment, thanks to his classmates and teachers. They had raised money for his trip.

Survival Equipment

CLIMBING SUIT—to protect against cold

GLOVES—to keep hands warm and dry

GOGGLES—to protect eyes from the sun's harmful rays and from reflection off snow

OXYGEN MASK AND TANK—for breathing at the highest altitudes

ICE AX—to help climb <mark>slopes</mark> and break up ice

CLIMBING ROPES—to climb up slopes

TREKKING POLES—to help a climber stay balanced

MOUNTAIN BOOTS—with spikes that dig into the snow and ice

Camp-to-Camp

Temba's second try began in April 2001. Mount Everest sits between Nepal and Tibet (tuh BEHT). There are several different routes to the top. Temba would take a route from the north, the Tibetan side.

Climbers move from one camp to the next higher one and then rest for a while. At each camp, their bodies get used to the higher altitudes. Temba spent several weeks moving between camps with his team.

At Camp 3, the team waited for a break in the weather. Winter was over, but there had been a series of severe snowstorms. Getting caught in a snowstorm farther up the mountain would be deadly.

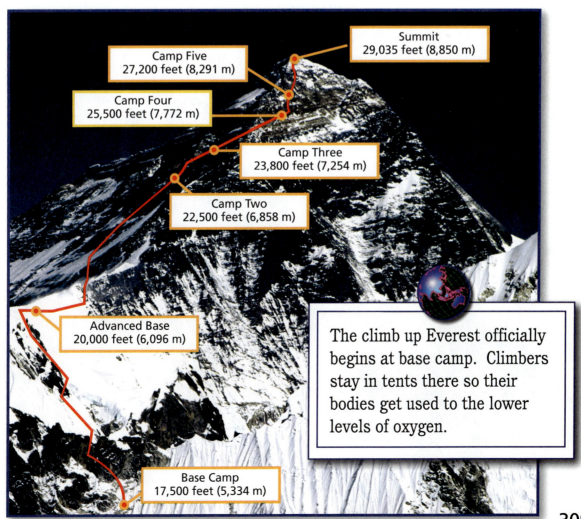

Summit
29,035 feet (8,850 m)

Camp Five
27,200 feet (8,291 m)

Camp Four
25,500 feet (7,772 m)

Camp Three
23,800 feet (7,254 m)

Camp Two
22,500 feet (6,858 m)

Advanced Base
20,000 feet (6,096 m)

Base Camp
17,500 feet (5,334 m)

The climb up Everest officially begins at base camp. Climbers stay in tents there so their bodies get used to the lower levels of oxygen.

The Climb Along the Ridge

On May 20, Temba's team reached Camp 4. Then the climbers headed out on the great ridge leading to the summit. Temba plunged his ax into ice walls, pulling himself up. He steadied himself against 50-mile-per-hour (80-kph) winds. Yet, he climbed higher and higher.

Temba had to move fast or die. Darkness stopped him before he got to Camp 5. His team had gone ahead. Luckily, Temba found a tent. He spent the night frightened and alone.

The next day, Temba rejoined his team. They reached Camp 6, one day's climb from their goal.

> **STOP AND THINK**
>
> **Author's Craft** Which words and details does the author use in this section to make the ridge climb sound dramatic and suspenseful?

Climbers have to be very careful. Towers of ice can fall over without warning.

Climbers use aluminum ladders to cross deep cracks in the ice, called crevasses. The crevasses are constantly opening and closing, so it is very dangerous.

Reaching the Top of the World

Just before midnight, Temba began his final climb. A headlamp lit the darkness. An oxygen mask helped Temba to breathe. Sometimes he'd stop to rest or to change oxygen bottles.

Just after sunrise, Temba reached Mount Everest's summit. He was higher than anyone else on the planet. Temba planted two flags. One was for his school. The other was for Nepal. "I felt so happy," he said.

It is dangerous for climbers to spend more than ten minutes at the top of Everest. The body needs to get to a lower altitude where there is more oxygen.

Temba was the youngest person to climb Mt. Everest.

Will the Mountains Survive?

Temba survived in the mountains. Now, he wants to make sure the mountains survive. The world's mountains face many different threats.

Trash is one problem. For a while, Everest was called the "world's highest garbage dump." The mountain was littered with tons of trash that climbers left behind—batteries, bottles, and empty oxygen tanks. Many climbers didn't have the time or strength to carry these things back down with them.

Climbers have left garbage on Everest since 1921. Now, people are trying to clean up the mess.

Global warming is another problem. As Earth gets warmer, mountain glaciers are melting. Himalayan lakes are swelling up with water. When they flood, mountain landscapes will be changed forever.

STOP AND THINK

Infer/Predict The author says Temba wants the mountains to survive. What do you think this means? What questions would you ask Temba to find out?

In 2005, the snowcap on Tanzania's Mount Kilimanjaro melted for the first time in history.

After the Climb

When Temba came down from Everest, he was thinking about food, not fame. After weeks of camping, he was starving for home cooking.

Still, when he flew home to Kathmandu, a huge crowd was waiting. Temba couldn't believe it. "I had never seen so many cameras. . . . All of them were pointed at me," he said.

Despite the attention, Temba focused on his schoolwork. He needed a good education to achieve his other dream, starting a school in Dolakha.

Will Temba <mark>succeed</mark>? Only time will tell. If you've survived on Everest, however, and reached the top, no goal seems too high!

Kathmandu (kat man DOO) is the capital and largest city of Nepal.

Temba smiled at supporters who greeted him at the Kathmandu airport after he successfully climbed Mt. Everest.

Your Turn

A Journey

Write a Response Why did Temba want to reach the top of Mt. Everest? Write a paragraph. Use details from the selection to support your answer. PERSONAL RESPONSE

Conquering Everest

Make a Plan Suppose you and your friends are a team of mountain climbers. Make a step-by-step plan for how you will climb Everest. Include a schedule and a list of equipment you will need. Take notes on the jobs each member of the team will do. SMALL GROUP

Fabulous Features

Turn and Talk Page through *Mountains: Surviving on Mt. Everest* with a partner. Discuss how each heading, map, and diagram adds to the text. Which features do you think are most useful? TEXT AND GRAPHIC FEATURES

THE BIG CLEANUP

by Kate McGovern

Cast of Characters

Scott, leader of the "Clean Everest" team

Talia, a team member

Rinzen, a guide from a nearby village

(A special team is preparing to climb Mt. Everest.)

Scott: Many people love to climb Mount Everest, but they leave behind trash. We're a new kind of climbing team. We're going up Mount Everest to help clean it up. Does everyone have his or her equipment?

Talia: (holding up her trash bags) We do. These bags are for carrying down trash.

Rinzen: We have oxygen in tanks. That's because air contains less oxygen as the altitude increases. It will be harder to breathe as we climb higher.

(They arrive at a campsite on the mountain.)

Scott: (looking around and frowning) Many climbers stopped here to rest as they approached the peak. They left old bottles, used batteries, and empty oxygen tanks.

Rinzen: Mount Everest should be one of the cleanest places on Earth.

Talia: Let's pick up the trash. Then the slopes will be cleaner.

Talia: We must be careful of avalanches up here.

Rinzen: That's right. An avalanche would bring our work to a halt.

Scott: (waving them onward) Let's go! This is the last section to climb. When we succeed, we will have climbed the tallest mountain on Earth.

Talia: We'll have collected lots of trash.

Scott: Other people are helping to clean Mount Everest, too. These days, climbers must bring drinks in cans. Then they flatten the empty cans and carry them away in their backpacks. If we all do our part, Mount Everest can stay clean for a long time.

Making Connections

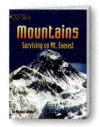

 Text to Self

Climbing a Mountain Would you like to climb Mt. Everest like Temba in *Mountains* or the characters in *The Big Cleanup*? Why or why not? Take turns telling a partner. Listen to each other and ask questions.

 Text to Text

Write a Play With a small group, write and act out your own short play in the style of *The Big Cleanup* about cleaning up trash on Mt. Everest. Include two facts from *Mountains* in your play.

 Text to World

Connect to Math Use details from *Mountains* to figure out how many years it was from the time Sir Edmund Hillary climbed Mt. Everest to the time Temba did. Hillary was born on July 20, 1919. How old was he when Temba reached the top of Mt. Everest?

Grammar

What Is a Preposition? A **preposition** connects words in a sentence. Prepositions can tell *where* or *when*. A **prepositional phrase** is a group of words that includes a preposition, a noun or pronoun, and words that describe that noun or pronoun.

Preposition	Prepositional Phrase
below	The clouds sit below the mountaintop.
during	The hiker lost eight pounds during the climb.
to	The climbers hike to the peak.
until	Temba waited until the storm passed.

 **Circle the preposition. Then underline the prepositional phrase in each sentence.**

1. Marty climbed up the long hill.

2. A heavy rain started during the hike.

3. Marty rested under some trees.

4. It was dry inside his tent.

5. He finished the hike by lunchtime.

Sentence Fluency Short, choppy sentences can be combined to make your writing smoother. You can combine two sentences by moving a prepositional phrase.

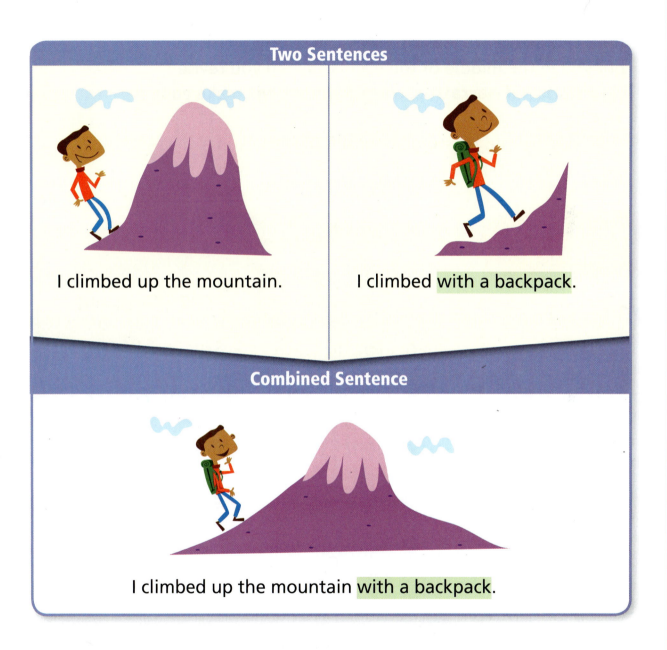

Two Sentences

I climbed up the mountain.

I climbed with a backpack.

Combined Sentence

I climbed up the mountain with a backpack.

Grammar in Writing

As you revise your story, look for places where you can combine sentences by moving a prepositional phrase.

Write to Express

☑ **Word Choice** Good writers try to make you feel what their characters are feeling. They use strong words to put you in the middle of the events. When you revise your **fictional narrative**, use words that will make your writing exciting.

Louis drafted his story about a family stuck in a sandstorm. Later, he added some stronger words.

Writing Process Checklist

Prewrite

Draft

▶ **Revise**

☑ Did I introduce the characters, setting, and problem in an interesting way?

☑ Does the middle part show how the characters deal with the problem?

☑ Does the end show how the problem works out?

☑ Did I use vivid words, details, and dialogue?

Edit

Publish and Share

Revised Draft

The sandstorm had been going on for ten hours. Sam and his parents ~~were~~ ^{hid} inside their covered wagon. The wind blew faster, ^{and louder} than Sam ever remembered. ~~It blew louder too.~~ The sand was ~~moving~~ ^{whipping} around them.

Sam and his family were moving out West.

Sandstorm!

by Louis Hudson

The sandstorm had been going on for ten hours. Sam and his parents hid inside their covered wagon. The wind blew faster and louder than Sam ever remembered. The sand was whipping around them.

Sam and his family were moving out West. Their wagon was full of everything they owned. There was barely enough room to sit. With the flaps closed, it was hot and stuffy inside. Sam poked his sweaty head out, but the sand stung him like insects. "How long will we have to wait?" he asked. His voice was shaky.

> In my final paper, I used stronger words to show how my characters felt. I also combined sentences.

Reading as a Writer

Which words show how Sam feels? Where can you make changes in your story to show what your characters are experiencing?

Our Awesome World

In this unit, you read about different kinds of journeys. When people take a journey, they learn about other people and places. Read the travel brochure below. Then choose a place you'd like to visit.

Feed the fish—or the alligators—at the Delta Rivers Nature Center as you discover why Arkansas's streams and wetlands are so important. ▶

Discover the Wonders of Wetlands

Whether you hike or take an airboat, the "river of grass" in Florida's Everglades is amazing. If you're lucky, you'll see a manatee or a Florida panther. ▼

Birdwatchers flock to the wetlands of Belize's Aguacaliente Wildlife Sanctuary. Visitors love to see the birds that make their home there. ▶

Collaborate

Think about what you read in the brochure on page 326. Then talk with a partner about these questions.

- ✔ Which place is most interesting to you? Why?
- ✔ Which place would you like to know more about? Why?
- ✔ What do you think you might learn?

Think Creatively

1. Do research on one of the places. Go online and learn more about it.

2. Then imagine you are visiting that place. Write a postcard to share what you see and learn.

Dear Uncle Pete,

I am visiting Belize. Yesterday I went to a wonderful wetlands.

postage stamp here

Mr. P. Lopez
2531 Pine Avenue
Little Rock, AR 72701

BELIZE

Unit 5 Wrap-Up

The Big 💡 Idea

Journey to the Future Write a page in your journal about a trip you take into the future. Tell about how you travel. Explain what you see and how life is different in 2060 than it is today.

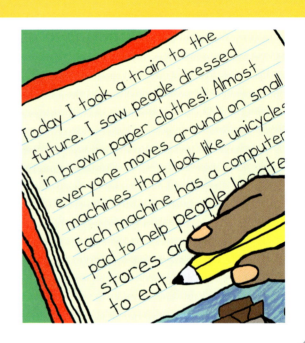

Listening and Speaking

Two Mountains Compare the pictures of mountains from two unit selections. First, look at the picture on page 179 of the mountain the two ants climbed. Then look at Mount Everest on pages 302 and 303. Tell a partner in what ways these mountains are alike and different.

Glossary

This glossary contains meanings and pronunciations for some of the words in this book. The Full Pronunciation Key shows how to pronounce each consonant and vowel in a special spelling. At the bottom of the glossary pages is a shortened form of the full key.

Full Pronunciation Key

Consonant Sounds

b	**bib**, ca**bb**age	kw	**cho**ir, **qu**ick	t	**t**igh**t**, s**t**opp**ed**
ch	**ch**ur**ch**, sti**tch**	l	**l**id, need**le**, ta**ll**	th	ba**th**, **th**in
d	**d**ee**d**, mail**ed**, pu**dd**le	m	a**m**, **m**an, du**mb**	*th*	ba**the**, **th**is
		n	**n**o, sudde**n**	v	ca**v**e, val**v**e, **v**ine
f	**f**ast, **f**i**f**e, o**ff**, **ph**rase, rou**gh**	ng	thi**ng**, i**nk**	w	**w**ith, **w**olf
		p	**p**op, ha**pp**y	y	**y**es, **y**olk, on**i**on
g	**g**a**g**, **g**et, fin**g**er	r	**r**oar, **rh**yme	z	ro**s**e, si**z**e, **x**ylophone, **z**ebra
h	**h**at, **wh**o	s	mi**ss**, **s**au**c**e, **sc**ene, **s**ee		
hw	**wh**ich, **wh**ere			zh	gara**g**e, plea**s**ure, vi**s**ion
j	**j**u**dg**e, **g**em	sh	di**sh**, **sh**ip, **s**ugar, ti**ss**ue		
k	**c**at, **k**ick, s**ch**ool				

Vowel Sounds

ă	p**a**t, l**au**gh	ŏ	h**o**rrible, p**o**t	ŭ	c**u**t, fl**oo**d, r**ou**gh, s**o**me
ā	**a**pe, **ai**d, p**ay**	ō	g**o**, r**ow**, t**oe**, th**ough**		
â	**ai**r, c**a**re, w**ea**r	ô	**a**ll, c**au**ght, f**or**, p**aw**	û	ci**r**cle, f**ur**, h**ear**d, t**er**m, t**ur**n, **ur**ge, w**or**d
ä	f**a**ther, ko**a**la, y**a**rd	oi	b**oy**, n**oi**se, **oi**l		
ĕ	p**e**t, pl**ea**sure, **a**ny	ou	c**ow**, **ou**t	yŏŏ	c**u**re
ē	b**e**, b**ee**, **ea**sy, p**ia**no	ŏŏ	f**u**ll, b**oo**k, w**o**lf	yōō	ab**u**se, **u**se
ĭ	**i**f, p**i**t, b**u**sy	ōō	b**oo**t, r**u**de, fr**ui**t, fl**ew**	ə	**a**go, sil**e**nt, penc**i**l, lem**o**n, circ**u**s
ī	r**i**de, b**y**, p**ie**, h**igh**				
î	d**ea**r, d**ee**r, f**ie**rce, m**e**re				

Stress Marks

Primary Stress ´: bi·ol·o·gy [bī **ŏl**´ ə jē]
Secondary Stress ´: bi·o·log·i·cal [bī´ ə **lŏj**´ ĭ kəl]

A

a·board (ə **bôrd´**) *adverb and preposition* On, onto, or inside a vehicle, such as a ship, train, or bus: *The captain welcomed us **aboard** as we stepped onto the ship's deck.*

ab·sorb (əb **sôrb´**) *verb* Take in or soak up: *A sponge can **absorb** lots of water.*

ac·ci·dent (**ăk´** sĭ dənt) *noun* An event that is not expected and not wanted: *Traffic was held up by two **accidents** on the highway.*

al·ti·tude (**ăl´** tĭ tōōd´) *noun* A height measured from sea level or from the earth's surface: *The plane flew at an **altitude** of 30,000 feet.*

an·chor (**ăng´** kər) *noun* A heavy metal object, attached to a ship, that is dropped overboard to keep the ship in place: *It took two sailors to raise the heavy **anchor** when the ship was ready to sail.*

an·cient (**ān´** shənt) *adjective* Very old; having existed for a long time: *They discovered an **ancient** treasure.*

an·nu·al (**ăn´** yōō əl) *adjective* Happening every year: *The **annual** town picnic is next week.*

ap·proach (ə **prōch´**) *verb* To come near or nearer: *As the storm **approached**, people were told to leave their seaside homes.*

ar·riv·al (ə **rī´** vəl) *noun* The act of reaching a place: *We waited for the **arrival** of our guests.*

av·a·lanche (**ăv´** ə lănch´) *noun* A large amount of snow, ice, or earth that falls down a mountain: *Skiers should be warned of the danger of **avalanches** on this mountain.*

B

base (bās) *noun* The lowest part; bottom: *We camped at the **base** of the cliff.*

bay (bā) *noun* A part of the sea that cuts into the land: *Have you ever seen sharks swimming in this **bay**?*

bur·y (**bĕr´** ē) *verb* Cover from view; hide: *I **buried** my face in the pillow.*

C

car·ton (**kär´** tn) *noun* A cardboard box used to hold goods: *Let's pack these gifts into a mailing **carton**.*

carton

ă r**a**t / ā p**ay** / â c**a**re / ä f**a**ther / ĕ p**e**t / ē b**e** / ĭ p**i**t / ī p**ie** / î f**ie**rce / ŏ p**o**t / ō g**o** / ô p**aw**, f**or** / oi **oi**l / ōō b**oo**k

chill·y (**chĭl´** ē) *adjective*
Unpleasantly cold: *Please
take a jacket if the weather is
damp and **chilly**.*

cli·mate (**klī´** mĭt) *noun* The
usual weather that occurs in
a place: *The **climate** in polar
areas is very harsh.*

clue (klo͞o) *noun* Something
that helps to solve a problem
or mystery: *Here are some
more **clues** to the riddle.*

clump (klŭmp) *noun* Thick
cluster or group: *Watch out for
clumps of poison ivy along the
path!*

col·o·ny (**kŏl´** ə nē) *noun* A
group of living things of the
same kind living or growing
together: *A **colony** of bees
built a hive in the tree.*

com·pli·ca·ted (**kŏm´** plĭ kā´
tĭd) *adjective* Not easy to
understand, deal with, or solve:
*Did you do the **complicated**
problem on page 5?*

con·stant (**kŏn´** stənt)
adjective Without a break
or pause: *The car is in
constant use.*

con·ver·sa·tion (kŏn´ vər **sā´**
shən) *noun* Informal talk
between two or more people:
*My sister has some long phone
conversations with her friends.*

cov·er·ing (**kŭv´** ər ĭng)
noun Something that covers:
*If it rains during our camping
trip, we can put waterproof
coverings on the tents.*

cur·rent·ly (**kûr´** ənt lē)
adverb At the present time;
now: *That movie is **currently**
showing.*

D

depth (dĕpth) *noun* Distance
from top to bottom or front
to back: *Crater Lake, with a
depth of over 1,900 feet, is our
deepest lake.*

des·ert (**dĕz´** ərt) *noun* A
dry area, usually covered with
sand, in which few plants or
animals live: *Animals that can
get by with little water often
live in **deserts**.*

dis·solve (dĭ **zŏlv´**) *verb* To
change from a solid to a
liquid: *To make hot chocolate,
dissolve sugar and cocoa
powder in hot milk*

dra·mat·ic (drə **măt´** ĭk)
adjective Exciting: *The
dramatic ending of the play left
the audience stunned.*

drip (drĭp) *verb* To fall or let
fall in drops: *Water is **dripping**
into the attic from a leak in
the roof.*

E

e·mer·gen·cy (ĭ **mûr´** jən sē)
adjective Giving urgent,
immediate action or care: *The
emergency animal hospital is
open all night.*

clue
Clue is sometimes
spelled *clew*. In
a Greek myth,
a prince named
Theseus was
jailed by King
Minos. To
escape, Theseus
had to enter a
maze, battle a
creature called
the Minotaur, and
find his way out
of the maze again.
Theseus used a
clew, a ball of
thread, to guide
him out of the
maze.

drip

---

o͞o b**oo**t / ou **ou**t / ŭ c**u**t / û f**u**r / hw **wh**ich / th **th**in / *th* **th**is / zh vi**si**on / ə
ago, sil**e**nt, penc**i**l, lem**o**n, circ**u**s

e·quip·ment (ĭ **kwĭp´** mənt)
noun The things that are
needed for a purpose: *This
store sells camping* **equipment**.

ev·i·dence (**ĕv´** ĭ dəns)
noun Facts or signs that
help one find out the truth or
decide: *The broken window
was* **evidence** *that a burglary
had taken place.*

ex·treme (ĭk **strēm´**)
adjective Very great: *The
Arctic explorers suffered from
the* **extreme** *cold.*

fiery

F

fierce (fîrs) *adjective* Wild
and savage; dangerous: *Tigers
can be* **fierce** *animals.*

fier·y (**fīr´** ē) *adjective* Of or
glowing like fire: *The* **fiery**
*red and orange sunset was
beautiful.*

fos·sil (**fŏs´** əl) *noun*
The remains or traces of a
plant or animal of an earlier
age: *These tiny* **fossils** *are the
bones of ancient birds.*

fright·en·ing (**frīt´** nĭng)
adjective Scary: *We spent
a* **frightening** *few minutes
listening to the bear outside
our tent.*

G

glass·y (**glăs´** ē) *adjective*
Smooth, clear, and shiny; like
glass: *We skated on the* **glassy**
surface of the frozen pond.

glide (glīd) *verb* To move
smoothly, quietly, and with
ease: *Many skaters were*
gliding *gracefully around the
ice rink.*

glob·al (**glō´** bəl) *adjective*
Worldwide; relating to the
entire earth: *Many countries
are cooperating in a* **global**
effort to end hunger.

guide (gīd) *verb* To show the
way to; direct: *The ranger*
guided *us along the park's
trails.*

H

halt (hôlt) *verb* To come or
bring to a stop: *Police will* **halt**
traffic to let the parade pass.

hard·ly (**härd´** lē) *adverb*
Barely; only just: *This box is
so heavy I can* **hardly** *lift it.*

hor·ri·fy·ing (**hôr´** ə fī´ ĭng)
adjective Causing strong fear
or horror: *Some nightmares
can be truly* **horrifying**.

ă r**a**t / ā p**ay** / â c**a**re / ä f**a**ther / ĕ p**e**t / ē b**e** / ĭ p**i**t / ī p**ie** / î f**ie**rce / ŏ p**o**t /
ō g**o** / ô p**aw**, f**o**r / oi **oi**l / o͞o b**oo**k

I

im·me·di·ate·ly (ĭ **mē´** dē ĭt lē) *adverb* At once; right away: *If you hear an alarm, leave the building* **immediately**.

in·crease (ĭn **krēs´**) *verb* To make or become greater or larger: *As your height* **increases**, *you usually gain weight, too.*

in·spire (ĭn **spīr´**) *verb* To move to action: *The promise of money* **inspired** *me to work hard.*

L

land·scape (**lănd´** skāp´) *noun* A stretch of land that is viewed as scenery: *We watched the desert* **landscape** *from the car window.*

la·va (**lä´** və) *noun* Melted rock that flows from a volcano: *Hot* **lava** *oozed down the side of the volcano.*

lay·er (**lā´** ər) *noun* A single thickness, coating, or sheet of material covering a surface: *Sprinkle a* **layer** *of cheese on top of the tomato sauce.*

lev·el (**lĕv´** əl) *noun* A certain height: *I waded in until the water was at chest* **level**.

liq·uid (**lĭk´** wĭd) *noun* A substance that flows easily: *Pour the* **liquid** *slowly into the flour and sugar mixture and stir well.*

load (lōd) *verb* To put into a vehicle or structure for carrying: *The dock workers* **loaded** *grain onto the ship.*

lo·ca·tion (lō **kā´** shən) *noun* A place where something is or can be found: *We finally found the* **location** *of the airport.*

love·ly (**lŭv´** lē) *adjective* Beautiful; very pleasing: *Their garden is the* **loveliest** *one I have ever seen.*

loy·al (**lo** i(-ə)l) *adjective* Faithful: *Shiva is a* **loyal** *friend, and I can always depend on him to help me.*

ly·ing (**lī** ing) *verb* Being in a flat or resting position: *Uncle Morris is* **lying** *on the couch, taking a nap.*

M

man·age (**măn´** ĭj) *verb* To succeed in doing something: *I* **managed** *to finish my work ahead of time.*

meas·ure (**mĕzh´** ər) *verb* To find the size, amount, capacity, or degree of: *Using a yardstick, Mom* **measured** *how tall we were each year.*

lava

The word *lava* comes from an Italian word. The Italian word, in turn, came from the latin word *labes*, meaning "fall."

measure

ōō b**oo**t / ou **ou**t / ŭ c**u**t / û f**u**r / hw **wh**ich / th **th**in / th **th**is / zh vi**s**ion / ə
ago, sil**e**nt, penc**i**l, lem**o**n, circ**u**s

G5

mi·grate (**mī′** grāt) *verb* To move regularly from one region or climate to another: *Many birds* **migrate** *south in the fall.*

mys·te·ri·ous (mĭ **stîr′** ē əs) *adjective* Very hard to explain or understand: *A* **mysterious** *light came from the empty house.*

N

nar·row (**năr′** ō) *adjective* Small or thin in width: *The road was long and* **narrow**.

O

o·ver·heat·ed (ō′ vər **hēt′** ĭd) *adjective* Too hot: *Pets can easily get* **overheated** *on hot summer days.*

P

pan·ick·ing (**păn′** ĭk ĭng) *adjective* Having a sudden feeling of great fear: *The* **panicking** *crowd pushed and shoved as they ran out of the building.*

part·ner (**pärt** nər) *noun* Someone who work or plays with one or more others: *The two* **partners** *took turns making and selling their lemonade.*

pas·sage (**păs** ĭj) *noun* Narrow pathway or channel: *Busy ants dig a maze of* **passages** *in each anthill.*

pa·trol (pə **trōl**) *verb* To move around an area in order to watch or guard: *Workers* **patrol** *the museum to make sure no one touches the paintings.*

pleas·ure (**plĕzh′** ər) *noun* A feeling of happiness or enjoyment; delight: *She smiled with* **pleasure** *when she saw the puppies.*

plen·ty (**plĕn′** tē) *noun* A full supply or amount: *Children need* **plenty** *of exercise.*

pol·len (**pŏl′** ən) *noun* Tiny grains that fertilize female plants to produce seeds: *Flower* **pollen** *makes new plants grow, but it also makes me sneeze all spring!*

pol·lu·tion (pə **lōō′** shən) *noun* The act of making dirty, impure, or harmful; the condition of being dirty, impure, or harmful: *Smog is a kind of air* **pollution**.

pre·his·tor·ic (prē′ hĭ **stôr′** ĭk) *adjective* Of, relating to, or belonging to the time before people began to record events in writing: *The bones of a* **prehistoric** *animal were found in a cave.*

ă r**a**t / ā p**ay** / â c**a**re / ä f**a**ther / ĕ p**e**t / ē b**e** / ĭ p**i**t / ī p**ie** / î f**ie**rce / ŏ p**o**t / ō g**o** / ô p**aw**, f**o**r / oi **oi**l / ŏŏ b**oo**k

proj·ect (**prŏj´** ĕkt´) *noun*
A plan for doing something;
scheme: *The town's voters
approved the building **project**.*

prove (prōōv) *verb* To show
to be true by backing up with
facts: *Getting an A on the test
will **prove** that you studied.*

puz·zling (**pŭz´** lĭng) *adjective*
Confusing; baffling: *I could
not put the toy together
because the directions were
so **puzzling**.*

Q

quiv·er (**kwi** vər) *verb* Shake;
tremble: *The squirrel began to
quiver with fear when my dog
got too close.*

R

re·cy·cle (rē **sī´** kəl) *verb* To
treat materials that have
been thrown away in order
to use them again: *Many
cities **recycle** glass, cans, and
newspapers.*

re·gion (**rē´** jən) *noun* A
usually large area of the earth's
surface: *This **region** receives
very little rainfall each year.*

re·mains (rĭ **mānz´**) *noun*
All or part of a dead body:
*The **remains** of this polar
bear were covered by ice for
hundreds of years.*

re·un·ion (rē **yōōn´** yən)
noun A gathering of the
members of a group who have
been separated: *Our family
has a yearly **reunion**.*

rip·ple (**rĭp´** əl) *verb* To form
or cause to form small waves:
*The surface of the river **rippled**
when I skipped a stone across it.*

rub·bish (**rŭb´** ĭsh) *noun*
Trash: *Please take this
rubbish out to the trash can.*

S

sci·en·tif·ic (sī´ ən **tĭf´** ĭk)
adjective Of, relating to, or
used in science: ***Scientific**
studies have shown that this
product works.*

scout (skout) *noun* Someone
who goes out from a group to
gather information: *The **scout**
returned to camp and told us
about the tracks he had found.*

sec·tion (**sĕk´** shən) *noun*
A part taken from a whole:
*A slice is a **section** of a cake
or pie.*

shade (shād) *noun* An area
that is partly dark because light
has been blocked off from it:
*It is too cold to sit in the **shade**.*

shel·ter (**shĕl´** tər) *noun*
Something that protects or
covers: *Stand under the
shelter at the bus stop if it's
raining.*

reunion
The word *reunion*
was formed
by joining the
Latin prefix *re-*,
meaning "again,"
with the Late
Latin word *unire*,
meaning "to
unite." Therefore,
reunion means
"to unite again."

section

ōō b**oo**t / ou **ou**t / ŭ c**u**t / û f**u**r / hw **wh**ich / th **th**in / *th* **th**is / zh vi**s**ion / ə
ago, sil**e**nt, penc**i**l, lem**o**n, circ**u**s

shift (shift) *noun* A scheduled period of work: *My brother works an early-morning shift at the restaurant.*

sin·cere (sĭn **sîr´**) *adjective* Honest; real; genuine: *Our feelings are sincere.*

skel·e·ton (**skĕl´** ĭ tn) *noun* The framework of bones in the body of a human being or an animal having a backbone: *People training to be doctors study skeletons to learn about human bones.*

slope (slōp) *noun* A stretch of ground that slants upward or downward: *The slopes on the hills behind our house are great for sledding.*

snap (snap) *verb* To bite or try to bite with a sudden motion: *A wild animal may snap at you if you try to pet it.*

sog·gy (**sô´** gē) *adjective* Soaked; very wet: *My shoe was soggy after the dog put it in the wading pool.*

sol·id (**sŏl´** ĭd) *adjective* Hard: *Those swans were carved from solid ice.*

spine (spīn) *noun* Part of a plant or animal that sticks out with a sharp point: *Porcupines are covered in prickly spines, or quills.*

spot (spŏt) *verb* To see, find, or locate: *The bird watchers spotted a huge woodpecker on their walk.*

store (stôr) *verb* Put away for future use: *Squirrels store acorns for winter.*

suc·ceed (sək **sēd´**) *verb* To carry out something desired or tried: *We will succeed at reaching our goal if we all work together.*

sum·mit (**sŭm´** ĭt) *noun* The highest point or part; top: *We rode a ski lift to the summit of the mountain and then zoomed down.*

sur·round (sə **round´**) *verb* To be on all sides of; encircle: *The people of the village built a wall that surrounded the whole town.*

sur·viv·al (sər **vī´** vəl) *noun* The act or fact of staying alive: *The family's survival is due to the firefighters' quick action.*

T

tank (tăngk) *noun* A container for holding or storing liquids or gases: *Divers always check to be sure that their tanks are filled with air.*

tem·per·a·ture (**tĕm´** pər ə chər) *noun* Hotness or coldness as measured on a standard scale: *The temperature is warmer in the sun than in the shade.*

ter·ror (**tĕr´** ər) *noun* Very great fear: *I screamed in terror as the roller coaster turned upside down.*

ă r**a**t / ā p**ay** / â c**a**re / ä f**a**ther / ĕ p**e**t / ē b**e** / ĭ p**i**t / ī p**ie** / î f**ie**rce / ŏ p**o**t / ō g**o** / ô p**aw**, f**o**r / oi **oi**l / o͝o b**oo**k

through·out (thrōō **out**´)
preposition In, to, or through every part of: *We walked* **throughout** *the city and saw all the sights.*

thun·der·ous (**thŭn**´ dər əs)
adjective Loud and rumbling: *A* **thunderous** *noise woke everyone up.*

trench (trĕnch) *noun* A long, narrow ditch: *The workers dug a* **trench** *and then laid pipes in it.*

trop·i·cal (**trŏp** ĭ kəl)
adjective From or typical of the tropics, the warm areas of Earth near the equator: *Mangoes and bananas are both* **tropical** *fruits.*

twist (twĭst) *verb* To wind together to form a single strand: *I watched as the woman* **twisted** *her long hair into a beautiful braid.*

U

un·a·ware (ŭn´ ə **wâr**´)
adjective Without knowledge of: *They were* **unaware** *that their actions were being recorded.*

un·cov·er (ŭn **kŭv**´ ər)
verb To reveal or remove the cover from: *Workers digging the tunnels are* **uncovering** *many objects from an earlier time.*

un·der·ground (**ŭn**´ dər ground´)
adjective Located below the surface of the ground: *An* **underground** *passage connects the two buildings.*

un·ex·pect·ed (ŭn´ ĭk **spĕk**´ tĭd)
adjective Taking place without warning: *We gasped when we heard the* **unexpected** *news.*

V

vi·o·lent·ly (**vī**´ ə lənt lē)
adverb With great physical force: *Waves crashed* **violently** *against the cliffs during the storm.*

voy·age (**voi**´ ĭj) *noun* A long journey made on a ship, aircraft, or spacecraft: *The astronauts will remember their* **voyage** *to the moon for the rest of their lives.*

W

wil·der·ness (**wĭl**´ dər nĭs)
noun An area in a wild, natural state in which there are no people: *You might see unusual animals and plants in a* **wilderness**.

with·in (wĭth **in**´) *preposition* Not going beyond the limits of: *We'll learn the results of the test* **within** *the next few days.*

underground
Underground is a compound word, or a word made from two or more shorter words. Compound words can be spelled as one word (*underground*), as two words (*air mail*), or as two words joined by a hyphen (*hard-boiled*).

ōō b**oo**t / ou **ou**t / ŭ c**u**t / û f**u**r / hw **wh**ich / th **th**in / *th* **th**is / zh vi**s**ion / ə
ago, sil**e**nt, penc**i**l, lem**o**n, circ**u**s

Acknowledgments

Main Literature Selections

The Albertosaurus Mystery: Philip Currie's Hunt in the Badlands by T. V. Padma. Copyright © 2007 by Bearport Publishing Company, Inc. All rights reserved. Reprinted by permission with Bearport Publishing Company, Inc.

"The Army Ants" from *Insectlopedia* by Douglas Florian. Copyright © 1998 by Douglas Florian. Reprinted by permission of Houghton Mifflin Harcourt Publishing Company.

Dog-of-the-Sea-Waves written and illustrated by James Rumford. Copyright © 2004 by James Rumford. All rights reserved. Reprinted by permission of Houghton Mifflin Harcourt Publishing Company.

Dogzilla by Dav Pilkey. Copyright © 1995 by Dav Pilkey. All rights reserved. Reprinted by permission of Houghton Mifflin Harcourt Publishing Company.

The Journey of Oliver K. Woodman by Darcy Pattison, illustrated by Joe Cepeda. Text copyright © 2003 by Darcy Pattison. Illustrations copyright © 2003 by Joe Cepeda. Reprinted by permission of Houghton Mifflin Harcourt Publishing Company.

The Journey: Stories of Migration written by Cynthia Rylant. Text copyright © 2006 by Cynthia Rylant. Reprinted by permission of The Blue Sky Press, a division of Scholastic, Inc.

"Knockabout and Knockaboom" from *A World of Wonders: Geographic Travels in Verse and Rhyme* by J. Patrick Lewis. Copyright © 2002 by J. Patrick Lewis. Reprinted by permission of Dial Books for Young Readers, A Division of Penguin Young Readers Group, A Member of Penguin Group (USA) Inc., 345 Hudson Street, New York, NY 10014, and Curtis Brown, Ltd.

Life on the Ice by Susan E. Goodman with photographs by Michael J. Doolittle. Text copyright © 2006 by Susan E. Goodman. Photographs copyright © 2006 by Michael J. Doolittle, except where noted. Reprinted by permission of Millbrook Press, a division of Lerner Publishing Group, Inc. All rights reserved.

"Mountain Mist/Neible del monte" from *From the Bellybutton of the Moon and Other Summer Poems/ Del ombligo de la luna y otras poemas de verano* by Francisco X. Alarcón. Copyright © 1998 by Francisco X. Alarcón. Reprinted by permission of the publisher, Children's Book Press, San Francisco, CA, www.childrensbookpress.org.

Mountains: Surviving Mt. Everest by Michael Sandler. Copyright © 2006 by Bearport Publishing Company, Inc. All rights reserved. Reprinted by permission of Bearport Publishing Company, Inc.

"A Mr. Rubbish Mood" from *Judy Moody Saves the World!* by Megan McDonald, illustrated by Peter H. Reynolds. Text copyright © 2002 by Megan McDonald, Illustrations copyright © 2002 by Peter H. Reynolds. Reprinted by permission of the publisher, Candlewick Press, Inc., and the author.

A Tree is Growing by Arthur Dorros, illustrated by S.D. Schindler. Text copyright © 1997 by Arthur Dorros. Illustrations copyright © 1997 by S.D. Schindler. Reprinted by permission of Scholastic Press, a division of Scholastic, Inc.

Two Bad Ants written and illustrated by Chris Van Allsburg. Copyright © 1988 by Chris Van Allsburg. All rights reserved. Reprinted by permission of Houghton Mifflin Harcourt Publishing Company.

"Until I Saw the Sea" from *I Feel the Same Way* by Lilian Moore. Copyright © 1967 by Lilian Moore. Reprinted by permission of the author c/o Marian Reiner, Literary Agent.

"Upside Down" from *When It Comes to Bugs* by Aileen Fisher. Copyright © 1986 Aileen Fisher. Reprinted by permission of the Boulder Public Library Foundation, Inc., c/o Marian Reiner, Literary Agent.

Credits

Photo Credits

Placement Key: (t) top; (b) bottom; (l) left; (r) right; (c) center; (bg) background; (fg) foreground; (i) inset.
TOC 4 t (c) Kevin Schafer/Corbis; **TOC 4** bkgd t age fotostock/SuperStock; **TOC 4** c (c) Jonathan Blair/CORBIS; **TOC 4** b Michael & Patricia Fogden/Minden Pictures; **TOC 5** t Photodisc/SuperStock; **TOC 5** c AP Photo/Sun-Times, Scott Stewart; **TOC 6** t WildPictures/Alamy; **TOC 6** b Getty Images/blue jean images RF; **TOC 7** t (c) Stapleton Collection/Corbis; **TOC 7** c Stuart Westmorland/Getty Images; **9** c (c) Brandon D. Cole/CORBIS; **10** cl Thinkstock Images/Jupiter Images; **10** cr (c) Getty Images; **10** bl Digital Vision/Getty Images; **10** br (c) Tom Grill/Corbis; **10** t (c) Kevin Schafer/CORBIS; **10** bkgd t age fotostock/SuperStock; **11** tl (c) Javier Larrea/age fotostock; **11** tc Paul Hurst/Alamy; **11** tr Stockbyte/Getty Images; **11** bl Bob Elam/Alamy; **11** bc Barry Mason/Alamy; **11** br (c) G. Baden/zefa/Corbis; **14** t Courtesy Candlewick Press; **14** Courtesy FableVision; **30** br imagebroker/Alamy; **30** tl (c) Kevin Schafer/CORBIS; **30** bkgd tl age fotostock/SuperStock; **30-31** bkgd age fotostock/SuperStock; **32-33** bkgd Edward Parker/Alamy; **31** br MICHAEL & PATRICIA FOGDEN/Minden Pictures; **31** tr (c) Kevin Schafer/CORBIS; **32** tr Michael & Patricia Fogden/Getty Images; **33** tr (c) Kevin Schafer/Corbis; **33** bkgd tr age fotostock/SuperStock; **37** br Rubberball/Jupiter Images; **38** cl (c) Tom Bean/CORBIS; **38** cr (c) Louie Psihoyos/CORBIS; **38** bl David McNew/Getty Images; **38** br (c) Louie Psihoyos/CORBIS; **38** t (c) Jonathan Blair/Corbis; **39** tl Louie Psihoyos/Getty Images; **39** tc Mark Wilson/Newsmakers; **39** tr (c) Richard T. Nowitz/CORBIS; **39** bl MICHAEL ANDREWS/Animals Animals - Earth Scenes; **39** bc blickwinkel/Alamy; **39** br (c) Garry Adams/Index Stock Imagery; **40-41** b Christian Jegou/Photo Researchers, Inc.; **42** Courtesy T.V. Padma;

Illustration